Becoming a Published Therapist

Becoming a Published Therapist
A Step-by-Step Guide to Writing Your Book

Bill O'Hanlon

W. W. Norton & Company
New York • London

Illustrations in this book by Diana E. Dube.

iPad is a trademark of Apple Inc., registered in the U. S. and other countries.

Amazon, Kindle, Kindle Fire, the Amazon Kindle logo and the
Kindle Fire logo are trademarks of Amazon.com, Inc., or its affiliates.

For information about permission to reproduce selections from this book, write to
Permissions, W. W. Norton & Company, Inc., 500 Fifth Avenue, New York, NY 10110

For information about special discounts for bulk purchases, please contact
W. W. Norton Special Sales at specialsales@wwnorton.com or 800-233-4830

Manufacturing by Quad Graphics Fairfield
Book design by Paradigm Graphics
Production manager: Leeann Graham

Library of Congress Cataloging-in-Publication Data

O'Hanlon, William Hudson.
 Becoming a published therapist : a step-by-step guide to
writing your book / Bill O'Hanlon. — First edition.
     pages cm
"A Norton Professional Book."
Includes bibliographical references and index.
ISBN 978-0-393-70810-3 (pbk.)
1. Psychotherapy—Authorship. 2. Medical writing.
3. Communication in medicine. I. Title.
RC437.2.O33 2013
616.89'14—dc23
                                        2012048357

ISBN: 978-0-393-70810-3 (pbk.)

W. W. Norton & Company, Inc., 500 Fifth Avenue, New York, N.Y. 10110
www.wwnorton.com

W. W. Norton & Company Ltd., Castle House, 75/76 Wells Street, London W1T 3QT

1 2 3 4 5 6 7 8 9 0

To Helen, who has written something deep on my heart.

Contents

Introduction:
"Stop Me Before I Write Again!"

I GOT THE CALL TO WRITE A BOOK SOME YEARS AGO. I had been presenting workshops for the previous seven years, and participants in my workshops had regularly begun to ask, "Where is your book?"

I would tell them I wasn't a writer. I had never had ambitions to write, although I loved to read. I didn't have much patience for sitting down and writing; I would rather speak. Also, I had no clue how to write a book or how to get it published.

Fast-forward 24 years. I have now written and published more than 30 books, many of them by mainstream firms such as W. W. Norton, the publisher of this book. One of my books got me on *Oprah*. My books have sold hundreds of thousands of copies all over the world. They have been translated into 16 languages.

How did I get from clueless to clued-in? How do you go from "I don't know how to write" to "Stop me before I write again"?

That's where you come in. You are probably reading this book because you have some curiosity about book writing and publishing or you wish to write a book and get it published. And because I wasn't a "natural writer" and was clueless about the process of both writing and publishing, I think I may be the perfect guide for you in realizing your writing dreams and goals.

I went to a "brown-bag" lunchtime presentation at a large psychotherapy conference some years ago, and the well-known presenter was giving a session on how to get a book published. She began by saying that an agent had learned of her work, approached her, and suggested she write a book. The book quickly became a best-seller. She admitted she really didn't know that much about getting an agent and getting published and that she had essentially fallen into best-sellerdom.

That certainly isn't my story. I worked at it by struggling to learn how to write and complete a book and then get it published. I think my journey is typical for most authors; in many ways, it's a hopeful message I have for you. Even if you are not a natural writer, even if you have no idea how to get a book published, it's possible to do both. I'll tell you exactly how to do so.

There are several components to the successful therapist/writer path:

1. Managing to find the time and discipline to write amid a busy life and practice;
2. Finding your writing style and voice;
3. Finding the intersection for your expertise, your passion, and the needs of the marketplace; and
4. Learning about and handling the business and marketing aspects of publishing in order to ensure that your book finds its intended readers.

If you are willing to engage in and accomplish each of these goals, the odds of getting your book written and published will increase.

I began to write in 1982. I was asked to be a guest editor for a journal issue, and, because I knew the editor wouldn't turn me down, I decided to write two articles for that issue. I wrote them on an electric typewriter (that should carbon-date me). It was very hard to write those articles: I avoided sitting at the typewriter; I was nervous and unconfident. When I finally began to write, I found my words to be flat and not at all reflective of what was in my mind or my heart.

I had to revise those first two articles again and again and still I didn't think they were well written. But they were good enough to publish in a clinical journal. (I actually met someone years later who told me they were his favorite articles in the issue, but they weren't my favorites, I can assure you.) That seemed to get me over the hump. I had become a published author!

This leads us to Lesson #1: Start writing and do what you can do to get anything published. This will help you think of yourself as a writer, thereby breaking that initial psychological barrier of not having been published. It will also help you begin to establish your writing "platform" (more on that later).

At a family therapy conference I attended, I met an acquiring editor, Susan Barrows, who ended up offering me a contract for my first book for W. W. Norton. In our initial discussion, I told her I was planning to write a book about Milton Erickson's work someday. She told me to keep her in mind when I did.

Lesson #2: Relationships, like in any endeavor, can help. People tend to think of the publishing industry in abstract terms, but for me it has mostly been about relationships with people. My current editor at W. W. Norton, Deborah Malmud, and I have an easy and good relationship that actually led to this book being written. Like with any relationship, if you are disagreeable, don't keep your word, or are demanding or entitled, don't expect to get far. Likewise, if an editor or agent in the publishing industry treats you badly or doesn't keep his or her word, ease out of that relationship as gracefully as you can.

I found the idea of writing a whole book quite daunting, so when a colleague in England (Jim Wilk) suggested we write a book together, I jumped at the chance, figuring that having a partner would be half the work. We got a contract offer from Guilford Press, a publisher that specialized in books for psychotherapists. I actually wrote many of my initial books with coauthors. Writing can be a lonely endeavor, and I find I keep my word to others better than if I make myself a promise to write or finish something by a certain time.

Lesson #3: Find a partner to write with if you find the task too daunting. Obviously, find someone who can pull his or her weight and who is able to work collaboratively.

It turned out that, due to Jim being in England (in the days before computers, email, and the Internet) and due to some personnel changes at Guilford, that first book, which was begun in 1983, didn't actually appear in print until 1987. By then, a book that I had done for W. W. Norton had been published.

Jim and I rewrote that book for Guilford 38 times! Because it was a first book for both of us, we wanted to get it right. Also, as I mentioned, I wasn't a very good writer and most of my final writing turned out to be rewriting. It took us the better part of three years to finish composing that book and then almost another year for it to be published.

Lesson #4: Traditional print publishing can take years. Be patient. Also, Lesson #5: Most good writing is the result of rewriting.

Eventually, I began to be faster and better at the book-writing process. After those first titles, each book generally took a year to write and rewrite. Later still, after many more publications, I found my writing and rewriting time was reduced to about three months per book.

After more than 30 books now, I usually write a book in a matter of weeks rather than in months or years. So I went from being a tortured, slow, not natural, or "good" writer to being a fast and relatively good writer. (I can always improve, and I still work on my writing skill regularly.)

Lesson #6: You will get better with more experience and practice.

One more note: This book is mostly about writing and publishing nonfiction, because that's what most therapists aim to do and that is also what I have experience and expertise in. Some of the material in the book also applies to writing and publishing fiction and will help in that endeavor, but fiction is a whole different kettle of fish and beyond the main scope of this book.

John Steinbeck wrote about avoiding the "hoptedoodle" some years ago. By that, he meant "fancy" writing that many readers glaze over or skip in a book. I have never been one for hoptedoodle, so enough of the preliminaries. Let's dive right in to the meat of the matter.

Becoming a Published Therapist:
A Step-by-Step Guide to Writing Your Book

CHAPTER 1

Why Would a Therapist Want to Write a Book?
Passion and Purpose

*I always wanted to be an author. I figured the way
to do that was to write a book.*

—Steve Martin

ONE CAN, I UNDERSTAND, HAVE A PERFECTLY FINE LIFE without
writing or publishing a book. I had one for 25 years before
my first book came out. Now, after more than 30 books, I can
barely remember life before having been published. But I was
not a natural writer. I struggled to write, and it felt like I spilled
blood on the keyboards in order to get each line down. When
I did write, I didn't like what I had written and had to rewrite
again and again so the books would be readable.

I also never grew up, as some do, with the dream of being
a writer. I liked to read, but it had never occurred to me to
write a book until I was an adult and felt that I wanted to
express something. Even then, I had no clue how to go about
writing or getting a book published.

Why might a therapist, in the midst of a busy life and practice, want to take the time to write a book and get it published?

I wrote my first books because I *had* to. Something inside
me insisted, and while I could have resisted the call, I knew

that I would be letting myself down as well as shirking an important contribution I could be making. So, I guess that is the first reason to write: because you feel you *have* to write.

Unlike me, some therapists are naturals and love the process of writing. Writing for publication, for those therapists, would be a way to get supported by doing something they enjoy or find satisfying.

After I began to get my books published, I had a colleague who also wrote who asserted that if one added up the time spent writing and revising, as well as dealing with publishers and getting the word out about the book, one ended up earning pennies per hour. I've never done the math, but either his books sell fewer copies than my titles or don't stay in print very long, because I still receive royalty payments from books I wrote in the 1980s, and I am sure it has worked out to be much more than pennies per hour for at least some of my published books.

So, another reason for therapists to write and publish books is to develop sources of passive income, that is, income that doesn't involve trading hours for money like most clinical work does. If my books continue on in print and continue to sell, I will have some supplemental income in retirement. You could too. As I write this, the financial system is still recovering from a severe downturn and many therapists who thought they would be able to retire from active practice have had to rethink their plans. Having supplemental income from book sales might be enough to free those therapists from their current location-based income and enable them to cut back or stop their practices a bit earlier. If not, it might help them pay a few bills or buy a few extras.

A book can also establish a therapist as a recognized expert in some area and can lead to other indirect increases of income. Since my first books came out, I have regularly received invitations to give paid speeches and workshops all around the world. In many years, I have made more money from public speaking than from my book royalties. That applies to coaching and consulting work as well. When your colleagues or readers start perceiving you as an expert, they will often want to hear more from you and may be willing to pay for you to share your knowledge.

Of course, just being recognized as an expert can be satisfying in its own right. I remember occasionally before I had any published books, I would have what I thought was an original idea, only to see it in someone else's book later or to hear some speaker saying something similar. I would kick myself for not having acted quickly enough to be recognized for that idea. Or I would read or hear something from one of the recognized experts in an area in which I had some knowledge and would think I had a better way of doing things or explaining things, but I would be frustrated because no one knew (or wanted to know) about my better way because I had no publications in that area.

That leads to one last reason why therapists might want to write and publish books: to have a positive impact on their field or on the world. The late Steve Jobs once exhorted his Apple cohorts to go out and "make a dent in the universe." Writing a book can be a way of leaving your mark.

I wrote this book to help therapists discover how to overcome their blocks to writing and publishing. I will discuss the inner and outer work of writing and publishing: overcoming procrastination and distraction, dealing with fears and writing blocks, and learning what works for you as a writer.

And I'll discuss how to get published. The publishing world, like any new territory, can be confusing and intimidating if you haven't lived in it or spent time learning about it. But like clients arriving confused and frightened for their first therapy session, once you engage in the process and learn a bit about the territory, it can become not only less frightening but also actually enjoyable.

I scrupulously avoided reading any books about the writing process when I began to write, because I knew I had the kind of personality that could forever be "fixin' to get ready," as they say down South. I worried that I would keep reading books about writing and not ever actually start writing.

But after my first five books were published, I allowed myself to read a few of them. None of them were exactly right for me, perhaps because I was mainly writing for a specialized audience of therapists, and perhaps because I had worked out my own way of writing and getting published. Still, I picked up a few helpful writing tips and learned more about the publishing industry, and so I am glad I read those books. Many years later, I began to teach and coach others to get their books written and published (I have helped authors to write and publish more than 100 books so far, which is pretty cool, I think). Because I was now teaching it, I began to read all the writing and publishing books I could. I have read most of them by now and have grabbed the best ideas from them to put into this book for you, combining them with my hard-won knowledge from 25-plus years of writing and publishing experience and what I have learned from coaching others.

I tried to make this book fun and chock-full of practical knowledge and guidance. My goal is to help you get your book (or books) written and published or at the very least to help you figure out that writing and publishing are not for you so you don't torture yourself about not having written a book.

I'll cover self-publishing, e-publishing, and getting published by traditional publishers (I've done them all), so you can decide which direction is right for you.

PASSION: FINDING THE ENERGY TO WRITE YOUR BOOK AND GET IT PUBLISHED

Passion for a book is like an electrical impulse traveling down a wire, and that electrical impulse has to be strong enough to affect a lot of people, from the writer to the agent to the editor. Then from the editor to the publicist who needs to get the book reviewed, the art director who is responsible for coming up with the right cover, the sales reps who sell the book to the store

buyers. Then from the store's main buyer to the individual book-sellers and, eventually, to the customer.
                —Lee Boudreaux, Senior Editor, Random House
                (quoted in *The Making of a Bestseller,* by
                Brian Hill and Dee Power [Chicago: Dearborn
                Trade Publishing, 2005])

It takes a good amount of effort to write a book and get it published (and then to get the word out to readers after publication). So I would suggest not starting on your writing project unless you have enough energy to pull you through the rough bits, the dips, the discouraging moments, and just the sheer amount of time it takes to see your book through to publication and get it successfully out into the world.

I always start my books when an idea moves me. I get energized about a topic. I have many ideas for books; I actually have outlines for about 10 or so books sitting on my computer hard drive as I write this. But I don't expand every idea into a book. But ideas aren't enough in my experience: The book must have some driving force that turns it from idea into action.

The essayist Annie Dillard writes this about the act of writing a book: "Writing a book is like rearing children—will-power has very little to do with it. If you have a little baby crying in the middle of the night, and if you depend only on willpower to get you out of bed to feed the baby, that baby will starve. You do it out of love. Willpower is a weak idea; love is strong. You don't have to scourge yourself with a cat-o'-nine-tails to go to the baby. That's the same way you go to your desk. There's nothing freakish about it. Caring passion-ately about something isn't against nature, and it isn't against human nature. It's what we're here to do" (from her essay "To Fashion a Text").

On the other hand, the best-selling business author Tom Peters was asked whether his book, *In Search of Excellence,* which caused a shift in business practices all over the world, was written for that express purpose. His response: "When I wrote [it] . . . I wasn't trying to fire a shot to signal a revolution. But I did have an agenda. My agenda was this: I was genuinely, deeply, sincerely, and passionately pissed off! (So what's the point? Just this: Nearly 100% of innovation—from business to politics—is inspired not by 'market analysis' but by people who are supremely pissed off by the way things are.)" So both positive and negative energies—what you love and what upsets you—can fuel one's writing.

In my view, there are four main energies you can tap into to write your book. The main writing energy you discover may be just one or you may find that you have a combination of more than one of these energies that fuels your writing endeavors. The four energies are Blissed, Blessed, Pissed, and Dissed. The first two represent the positive energies; the last two, the "negative."

Blissed is the excited, deeply joyful energy that some people get when they think of or pursue certain endeavors in life. If you love music and it brings you to a state of ecstasy regularly, music may be your bliss. Or it may be a certain kind of music, perhaps punk rock, reggae, jazz, dance, or classical. Or perhaps extreme sports do it for you. Or maybe it is movies that turn your crank. I'm not talking about addictive substances here, though, but it is whatever you can't get enough of: not what merely feels good or tastes good in the moment, but something that is deeply soul satisfying or fulfilling. You can tell what blisses you out by what kinds of things you can't keep yourself from doing, thinking about, or sharing with others.

The filmmaker George Lucas put it this way: "You have to find something that you love enough to be able to take risks, jump over the hurdles, and break through the brick walls that are always going to be placed in front of you. If you don't have that kind of feeling for what it is you're doing, you'll stop at the first giant hurdle."[1]

1. "A Life Making Movies," *Achievement.org*, October 14, 2010, www.achievement.org/autodoc/page/luc0int-2

There is a Hasidic saying I came across: *Everyone should carefully observe which way his heart draws him and then choose that way with all his strength.* This is the way of following your bliss into writing.

Blessed involves people or situations that have bestowed grace or encouragement on you in life. Perhaps you had a friend who believed in or encouraged you. Or a parent or grandparent told you that you could do anything that you set your mind to or that you were smart or talented. Or a colleague has always encouraged you to follow your dreams. There may have been a customer or client who responded so positively to something you did that it gave you a new sense of direction or confidence, or an English teacher who told you your writing was good and that you should consider pursuing publication. When that person blessed you with confidence in yourself or with his or her encouragement, it released a certain energy and pointed you in some direction, perhaps, to apply that energy.

Early on in my career, my younger sister, who attended the same university as I did, asked me to be on a panel for a women's organization she headed. The topic was feminism and psychotherapy. I was the only male on the panel, but it all went well. Afterward, my sister came up to me and told me she was astonished at what a good job I had done (I had been very shy as we were growing up and hadn't been a very talkative person). She told me that I should be on some national talk show like *Donahue* or *Oprah*. I was astonished by that comment, but over the years, she continued to prod me to get my work out in a big way. She believed in me. When I was invited to appear on Oprah with my book *Do One Thing Different* many years after my sister's initial comment, she was the first person I called. She took it all in stride and told me that while she was excited, she had always known it would happen one day. She is a person who blessed me and helped steer me in the direction of speaking and writing.

The paranormal mystery writer Charlaine Harris was blessed by a husband who believed in her, perhaps more than she believed in herself. He gave her an electric typewriter on their wedding day, suggested she quit her job, and said, "I know you've always wanted to write. Try staying home and writing the book you've always wanted to write." She avoided writing for several months after that but he gently nudged her to begin. She did so and has turned out many successful novels, one series of which has now been made into a popular television show, *True Blood.* Not all writers are blessed with such encouraging partners.

You might have been blessed with inborn talents or sensibilities that serve you well. Some people have a great sense of color or aesthetics. Some people have a natural talent for art. Some people find they can organize ideas or physical objects. Others have a talent for connecting with people.

Another blessing is to be in the right place at the right time. Perhaps you were an artist or writer in Paris in the 1920s or 1930s. Perhaps you were a rock-and-roll musician in Memphis in the 1950s. Or you met someone who changed your life through a random meeting. That happened for me when I met the psychiatrist Milton Erickson while I was working at the Matthews Art Gallery at Arizona State University. I ended up becoming his student (and gardener, because I couldn't afford to pay him). He mentored me and changed the course of my career and my life. I went on to write several books about his work and many more that were inspired by his spirit and approach. I later edited the Milton Erickson Foundation newsletter, which led to some international speaking opportunities and to my first book contract offer. Luck, serendipity, fate, whatever you call it: I was blessed to be in the right place at the right time to meet Dr. Erickson.

Pissed (meaning "pissed off" in this context, but shortened to rhyme with blissed and dissed) refers to the stuff in life that upsets you, gets you angry, or makes you righteously indignant. Many of my early books were written from a combination of pissed and blissed. I was excited about a certain approach to helping people change in psychotherapy but also, frankly, pissed off about what I perceived as some discouraging and disrespectful approaches in vogue at the time I became a therapist. I wrote my books to change people's minds.

I heard an interview on Barnes and Noble's audio interview podcast with Andrew Vachss, a writer who used to be a federal prosecutor of criminals who committed sex crimes against children. He says he got so angry after seeing what was done to children in our society that he decided he had to write to get a bigger jury and to change people's minds so that laws about parents' ownership of children would change. "I didn't go to prep school," he said, noting that he had grown up in a tough section of New York City. "I saw things that not only nobody should see, but things that shouldn't exist." The root of it all, he worked out, was this idea that parents owned children and could do what they wanted with them and that parents felt society would protect their rights because they were "parents." He had one perpetrator tell him matter-of-factly, "Of course I sodomized my baby, but that is *my* baby." Vachss wanted to kill the man at that moment, but he knew that wouldn't change things for the other children, so he began to write novels that were engaging but had the underlying message of the evils of declaring that parents owned children. He was tapping into being pissed to write.

Another writer who used angry energy to write was the author J. A. Jance. When she tried to enter a creative writing class in the 1960s, the professor told her that "girls don't become writers" and that she should become a teacher or nurse instead. Jance's then husband was also an aspiring writer and he declared, "There will only be one writer in this family, and it's me."

Some years later, after divorcing and becoming a single parent, Jance got up at 4:30 a.m. daily to write for several hours before her kids awakened and she had to get them to school before going to her job. What do you think gave her the energy to get up so early and persist in her writing until she got published? She was pissed. (She got her revenge in print. She made one character in the book a husband who drank too much and declared himself the only writer in the family and actually never published anything, and she made the crazed killer a creative writing teacher.) The best-selling mystery writer Sue Grafton did something similar after she went through a terrible divorce in which she got legally trounced in a very unfair way. After spending time fantasizing about the perfect undetectable way of killing her ex, she decided to do it in print, leading to her first best-seller, *A Is for Alibi*.

Dissed means two things: dissatisfied or disrespected. This refers to the areas of life in which you were or someone you care about was disrespected or treated badly. It also refers to those areas in which you are dissatisfied with the status quo, including times when you were wounded, hurt, or trauma- tized. Being wounded in a certain area can help you be more sensitive to others who have suffered or are suffering similar hurts. Martin Luther King was moved to social action by being disrespected and by seeing people he cared about disre- spected. People often start businesses when they can't find the product or services they want and are dissatisfied enough to do something about it.

Follow Your Wound

A variation on this dissed energy is being wounded. Many get sensitized and energized to some book topic due to some disrespect or hurt or a psychological wound they have suffered.

The novelist Anne Rice's 5-year-old daughter died of leukemia. She grieved mightily, of course, but when the time came to go back to her work as a legal assistant, she found she just couldn't do it, even though her family needed the income. Her husband suggested that she delay going back to the office and work on that novel she had always wanted to write. The novel that emerged from that period was a compelling dark novel about vampires called *Interview With the Vampire*. It featured a 5-year-old character who became a vampire (and therefore could never die). Rice imbued this character with all the qualities and features of her dead daughter, in the hopes of never forgetting those aspects of her as time marched on.

The dismissive thing that is often said about psychotherapists is that they only become therapists to try to heal themselves and to work out their own problems or fix their families. While that may have some truth to it in many cases, I think a more nuanced and complete way of saying it would be that many therapists find their way to the profession because they were hurt, disrespected, or wounded in some way that sensitized them to the pain, problems, and suffering in a particular area.

My friend, Michele Weiner-Davis, the author of *Divorce Busting* and other books about helping keep couples together even when it looks like their marriages or relationships are over, suffered from her own parents' bitter divorce when she was young. Her books have helped countless couples stay together and have better relationships. She was so energized because she had personally experienced and witnessed the suffering that can accompany breakups, and she saw that many therapists were cavalier about whether or not the couple stayed together, while some actually encouraged divorce in situations that Michele felt would not be necessary.

I was molested as a child and therefore I have been sensitized to this issue, and it has led to my writing several books about trauma recovery and resilience as well as directly about treating the aftereffects of sexual abuse.

Here is another story to illustrate the notion of how a wound can fuel writing and passion.

My colleague Ernest Rossi, like me, studied with Milton Erickson. One time, at a large conference devoted to Erickson's work, Ernie and I sat down to chat about what had brought us to study with Erickson. Ernie told me that when he was growing up, he had a learning disability (they didn't know about such things in those days) that made it difficult for him to learn to read. When he fell seriously behind the other children, he was taken out of his classes and put with the kids who were at that time called "retarded." His former classmates were merciless, as kids can be, teasing him on the playground, chanting, "Ernie's a retard, Ernie's a retard." He was terribly ashamed. Sometime later he finally learned how to read and rejoined his old classmates, but they never forgot and continued their playground taunts. When Ernie entered high school, his family had moved, and he had a chance to escape his old shame. But on that first day of high school, he began to doubt himself. *Maybe I'm not smart enough to hack it in high school*, he thought. After classes, he wandered around the big library at the school, feeling overwhelmed by all the knowledge contained in those books. His attention was caught by one particularly thick tome. *If I could ever read a book like that and understand it*, he told himself, *it would prove I wasn't stupid.* He plucked it out of the stacks and read the title: *A Critique of Pure Reason*, by Immanuel Kant. He sat down to read it. He read the first paragraph and could not make heads or tails of it. He read it again and again and again until he finally understood what the author was saying. He did the same with the first page and finally, after understanding it, walked home with a feeling of satisfaction. Ernie visited the library every day after school and read that book until he had understood the entire thing. He read the book three times by the end of high school.

Ernie went on to college and graduate school. He was pursuing his Ph.D. in pharmacognosy (don't ask: it has to do with plants and medicines) when a fellow Ph.D. student came to him one day and thrust a book in his hand and said, in effect, *Ernie, you are really messed up and need to read this book. It will help you.* Ernie looked up from his microscope, puzzled, and examined the thick book: *The Interpretation of*

Dreams by Sigmund Freud. He took the book home, opened it, and immediately fell under its spell. Ernie is a very intro-verted guy and has a rich inner life. Here was a map of that inner life. The book completely captured him, so much so that he read it again and again (sound familiar?). Ultimately, he decided to drop out of his pharmacognosy program and to get a Ph.D. in psychology. He went on to become a Jungian analyst. Ernie created a new method of working with dreams, wrote a book about it, and developed a successful practice in Southern California.

Things were going along fine until some of his patients told him that when he had been doing dreamwork with them, they felt that they had gone into trances. Ernie was upset by this. He was doing Jungian work and considered hypnosis to be a cheap parlor trick. But, as time went on, more and more patients mentioned this to him. One day, one of Ernie's most respected patients, a wise older man who knew a lot about Jungian work, also mentioned that Ernie's dreamwork was very hypnotic. When they discussed it, the man said he had a book Ernie should read. He dropped the book off that day: *Advanced Techniques of Hypnosis and Therapy: Selected Papers of Milton H. Erickson, M.D.*, edited by Jay Haley. Ernie took the book home at the end of the day (a Friday). As before, he opened the book curiously and again found himself captured. Erickson had an amazing way of working, which was entirely different from the way Ernie had been taught. He spent all weekend reading the book. He was so excited about what he was reading that he barely slept until Sunday night.

When he awoke on Monday morning, Ernie had a severe stomachache. It was so painful that he went to the emergency room, where he was admitted and put through many tests. The tests found no physical cause for the pain, and Ernie and the doctors finally concluded that it must be psychosomatic. With the help of some medication, Ernie was able to return to his practice. When the patient who had lent him the book came for his appointment, Ernie told of his excitement about reading the book and of his subsequent stomach problems. Since the book, written several years previously, had suggested that Erickson was ill and would soon die, Ernie told his patient that it was too bad that Erickson was dead or he would have sought therapy from him. The man informed Ernie that Erickson had recovered from his illness and was living in Phoenix.

Soon Ernie was on the phone to make an appointment with Erickson. As he was driving from California to Phoenix, his stomach pain disappeared. He arrived and told Erickson his story, and they decided that Ernie would study with Erickson. They ultimately worked together on three books in which Ernie explained in detail how Erickson did what he did. Ernie has gone on to write many books about Erickson's work and about mind-body healing and related topics.

My point is that, in some ways, Ernie's life work and his writing so many books derived mainly from his pain and self-doubt. He seems to have proved by now (in his 70s) that he is not stupid (he assured me recently that he finally settled the issue within himself in his late 50s when he found that he had mastered some advanced mathematical ideas none of his bright friends could even come close to understanding), but he followed both what upset him (proving he wasn't stupid by persisting with difficult material; following his stomachache to Erickson; mind-body healing) and his bliss (dreams and Erickson's work).

Defeat Your Curse

Another variation on the dissed energy is cursed. Who has discouraged you or made negative predictions about you or your writing?

I read the actor and comedian Billy Connolly's biography. He grew up in Scotland and was a very poor student, in part due to some unrecognized learning problems. His teachers beat him and generally humiliated him in front of the other students. When he became a successful film star and internationally renowned comedian, he used to drive by those former teachers' houses and feel a smug satisfaction that he had proven them wrong in their prediction that he would grow up to be a failure and worthless.

Who has put a curse on you by putting you down or making negative prognostications about your future? And how did you respond to those curses, put-downs, or negative predictions? Did they fuel your desire to prove those people wrong or are you still living under the curse?

My friend and colleague Steve Gilligan's father's regular put-down of him was "Who the hell do you think you are?" When, many years later, as an adult, Steve sat down to write his first book, he was stopped by a recurring doubting voice in his head that asked the same question: *Who the hell do you think you are that you could write a book?* It took Steve some time to find a way to overcome that curse and to find his way to publication.

Dissatisfied is when the energy you have might not be as strong as when you are pissed, but it could still lead to a desire to write about some situation that dissatisfies you.

Some years ago, I visited the well-known therapist Albert Ellis. He had written too many books to count, perhaps more than 100. He created a major shift in therapy, starting in the 1950s. At the time I met him (in March 2000), he was in his 80s and was still working 70-plus hours per week. When I asked him what drove him to do what he had done in his career, he said that he couldn't stand the inefficiency of therapy and wanted to make it work better. He had learned psychoanalysis, the dominant model of therapy at the time (1950s) and it bothered him because it didn't work very well and took years. He told me that if he hadn't become a therapist, he probably would have been an engineer because he liked to make things more efficient. Then came 50 years of nonstop activity, initially all because psychoanalysis annoyed him. After he began to practice his new way and to teach and write about it, he found he enjoyed it, so he kept doing it.

Those then are the four energies that can power your writing. The novelist Jane Smiley, in a 2006 interview in *Writer's Digest*, also emphasized the need for finding the energy to sustain your writing life: "You have to have a lot of energy and conviction to propel yourself through the writing of a novel, because it often takes a year, two years, or more. So the interest has to be a compelling one. And lots of times the reason the subject is compelling is because you have passionate convictions about it. Most prolific writers are, by nature, people of passionate ideas, but the particular ideas that make them passionate tend to come and go over the years. They keep going by taking up new ideas with the same passion."

Since I am now on my 30th or so book, I can relate to that. I get passionate, sometimes so excited I can barely contain myself, other times so upset I want to change the world. I have different enthusiasms now than I did when I started writing a quarter of a century ago, but I am still enthusiastic. When the energy is gone, I will happily retire from the writing life and let more passionate people take over.

FEAR: THE FORCE THAT CAN BLOCK YOUR WRITING ENERGY

Having coached so many people to write and get published, I have learned that fear is pretty common out there when it comes to writing and getting published. Most people fear being so public, being exposed, being vulnerable. They fear being criticized. They fear looking foolish. They fear failing. Fear has stopped many from even starting their writing or has kept them from completing their books or getting them published.

Because most who are reading this book are therapists, my target readers, they probably have some skill in both recognizing and dealing effectively with fear. As a therapist, you might draw on that skill if you need it for yourself now in getting your book written, completed, and published.

How would you work with clients or patients who are afraid of something? They either avoid that area or they catastrophize about the potentially bad things that might happen. How do you get them past that?

If you have some helpful ideas or methods, use those right now with yourself to identify and to begin to move beyond fear in regard to your book and its publication. Or you could just begin writing about the thing you are afraid to write. That will at least get you writing and may help clarify or perhaps move you through the fear. Fear can be thought of as "frozen energy"; perhaps the heat of attention to it may help melt it and release that energy to be available for your writing.

Or you might just write what you are afraid to write, and you promise yourself you will keep it private and unpublished. This containment may be enough to break the dam and get you to write and express what you are afraid to put on paper. After that, things may shift with other writing or you may find a way to make the forbidden, feared material publishable.

In a later chapter, we will get into the writing process and I'll have more to say about overcoming writing blocks and fears. For now, please take some time and fill out the following worksheet. Because this is the first worksheet of many, let me give some introductory remarks. All the worksheets are included on the DVD that came with this book as well as being on the website, so you can download them as Word files.

Typically, when I come across worksheets or exercises in a book (or a workshop), I don't do them. So, I sympathize with you if you feel the same way. But I do recommend you take the time to actually work on and complete these worksheets and exercises. I didn't include them for filler. And doing them will significantly move you forward on your writing and publishing journey. These worksheets and exercises have been road-tested with hundreds, perhaps thousands, of people, and they have helped many get clear and get moving. So if you can, please do the worksheets.

Okay, now we move on to the worksheet that can help you find the energy to sustain you through your writing project.

✏️   Passion Worksheet   ✏️

What Energizes You?

Pissed. Write down what you hope your book will do to change people, the world, or your field.

Wounded. Write about a wound that you want to educate or sensitize others to or to keep from happening to others by getting your book out into the world.

Blissed. Write down what you are excited about that you want everyone to know through your book.

Blessed. Write down how you have been blessed. By whom have you been blessed? What circumstance have you lived or been born into that could be a blessing?

Fear. Write down what you are afraid to write but that you know is the deep truth. That fear is either blocking you from writing or writing with all your energy, uniqueness, and power. What would you write about if you weren't afraid or ashamed?

Coming at this same material from a different angle, I offer a set of questions that may clarify why you are writing and what energy (or energies) will keep you moving through the process of completing your book. Again, please take the time and energy to engage in these to get the maximum benefit from them.

Identifying the Fueling Energy for Your Book

What turns you on, blisses you out, excites you, or compels you?

What do you seek out without any prodding from guilt or duty?

What are you obsessed with in a soulful (not in an unhealthy or addicted) way?

What are you passionate about?

What do you care about so deeply or get so excited about that you talk about it to anyone who will listen?

Do you love the process of writing itself?

Who has encouraged your writing or self-expression?

What pisses you off?

What has hurt you so much that you want to prevent it from happening to others?

What would you talk about if they gave you an hour of prime-time television in which you could address the nation?

What injustice do you want to correct or prevent?

Who would be proved wrong if you succeeded as a writer?

Who has criticized, cursed, or discouraged you to the extent that it makes you want to prove them wrong?

What upsets you so much that you are compelled to write about it or include it in the theme of your book?

When have you (or someone you cared about) been disrespected or treated in a way that makes you want to write?

Where have you been lucky enough to be in the right
place at the right time in regard to your writing?
What are you afraid to write that you know is a deep
truth or something you should write about?
Who are you afraid will disapprove of your writing or be
upset by it?
What are you afraid will happen if you write?
What fears could you write about and perhaps work
through by writing?

Key Points

- There are many potential benefits for therapists in writing
and publishing a book: establishing yourself as a recognized expert; getting greater visibility, which can help
your clinical practice; developing a supplemental income
source that can extend even into retirement; and making
a positive contribution to the world with your hard-won
knowledge.
- In order to write a book and sustain yourself through
writing, editing, publishing, and marketing, you need
energy.
- Find the particular energy (blissed, blessed, pissed, or
dissed) or a combination of energies that are fueling your
desire (or compulsion) to write a book.
- If you find that fear is blocking you, consider it as frozen
energy and find some way to unfreeze that energy.

CHAPTER 2

Getting Clear on Your Topic and Direction
Problem, Promise, Population, Positioning, and Program

*The most important thing in a work of art is that it should
have a kind of focus, i.e., there should be some point where
all the rays meet and from which they issue.*

—Leo Tolstoy

THE BOOKS THAT I HAVE WRITTEN but haven't published have
failed to find a publisher because they are not clearly thought
through. I haven't narrowed down and specified the audience for whom I am writing the books. Or I haven't clearly
differentiated the books from others that have already been
published.

I have heard from publishers more than once with the
following rejection: This book has already been written. (Like
my parents heard more than once from my teachers, "Bill's not
working up to his potential.") I hate to hear this, but what I
have learned is that I haven't done enough work upfront clarifying and thinking through what the book is about and that I
haven't focused the book enough.

If you are seeking a publisher, you are most likely to be
rejected for two reasons: You don't have a clear-enough focus
or a big-enough platform. In this chapter we will work on
the focus part, so that it never becomes a block to finding

a publisher or readers for your book. The literary agents Jeff Herman and Deborah Levine Herman wrote, "Having a focused idea is imperative. An unfocused idea is one of the main reasons why a book proposal will be rejected" (p. 10).

To make the elements of clarifying and focusing your book more memorable, I have come up with several P words to describe the main elements:

- Problem
- Promise
- Population
- Program/Prescription
- Positioning

In addition to Passion, which was covered in the last chapter, these constitute the core of your book-writing process. If you don't have these elements clearly thought out and articulated, your book will likely have trouble finding a publisher and an audience. If you do think them through, you are likely to succeed.

Often, would-be authors get caught up in their own perspective, enamored with the great idea about which they are so excited but neglecting to think about their audience—the readers.

Passion is a great place to start, but the next step is to shift the attention away from yourself and out into the world, into the minds and interests of publishers, agents, and editors (if you want someone else to publish your book) and to the readers.

These Ps are designed to ensure that your book is focused and sellable once you have connected with your own energy. In this phase of preparing your book, your energy and attention should be turned outward rather than inward.

People send me book proposals and manuscripts all the time to evaluate and to ask me why they haven't been able to be published. Most of the time, these are of interest only to the author and perhaps a few of his or her family and friends.

The book may be full of life details with no indication as to why readers who don't know the person should care about these details. This kind of writing might be personally satisfying, but it isn't commercial or appropriate for a wide readership.

To ensure that your book is relevant and of interest, you need to see it through the reader's eyes, not your own. This chapter will help you do that.

THE PROBLEM

Books must solve problems for readers. Even if the book is a novel, it must solve a problem or fulfill a goal, or the reader won't bother to pick it up and read it.

In nonfiction books, the problem is often a life problem or dilemma. People want to know how to save money or have better relationships. In fiction, it may be that characters are bored or want some excitement in their lives. (As I write this, a book about an S&M relationship [*Fifty Shades of Grey*] is popular among suburban housewives, and a young adult novel about teens forced to kill one another in a nationally televised event [*The Hunger Games*] is the best-selling book in the United States. These books take people away from their humdrum everyday lives into other worlds of novelty.)

Therefore, your first task in clarifying your book topic is to figure out what problem you will solve for your readers. Will you help them reduce or eliminate anxiety or depression? Will you help them get through a divorce with minimal damage? Will you help them stop being broke?

There are two basic things that motivate people as far as I can tell:

1. Things that cause them discomfort that they would like to avoid, reduce, or eliminate in their lives. Put more simply: What do they complain about? We can call this "negative motivation."

2. Things they would like to have or have more of in their lives. This can be called "positive motivation." Again, put simply, what do they want?

Your book should deal with one or both of these in order to motivate people to buy it (and publishers to publish it). Offer your potential readers a solution that involves getting rid of discomfort or offering something to which they aspire.

Therapists sometimes get enamored with the approach they use: schema therapy, cognitive-behavioral therapy, Gestalt psychology, solution-focused therapy. But people who read your book really want a problem solved; they usually don't care as much about the exact way you will go about solving it as that you can help them with their problem.

One useful tool in this regard is provided for free by Google, the search engine service. Google lets people research what terms other people are typing into the search engine to find answers, solutions, or information (this helps advertisers find their market more precisely, which helps Google make more money). The free tool is called Keyword Tool and you can find it by searching Google for it. Once there, put in some search terms of problem phrases that you think people might be searching in your target area, such as "divorce" or "panic attacks." Then dig down from there and see what phrases and words people search for most often. This may change your focus slightly and even the name of your book.

For example, when I dig down into the search term "panic attacks" by using this Google tool, I find that phrases people are searching for include "what causes panic attacks," "panic attack treatments," "overcoming panic attacks," and "how to treat panic attacks." All of these phrases could help you find a good title for a book or a section of your book: suddenly you don't have to guess. You can do some quick research in the real world (okay, the cyber world) and come up with a strategy.

✐   The Problem Worksheet   ✐

This is the problem that my potential readers are concerned about:

This is something my readers really want to avoid or get away from:

This is something my readers really want to have but they don't have or they don't know how to get it:

This is my argument and my statistics or data, which will convince readers that they need to read my book:

These are the Google search terms and phrases people are typing in to find information or solutions for this problem:

THE PROMISE

What I have called here "the promise" (a solution) goes hand-in-hand with the problem that your book will help to solve. This is like spelling out the benefits in marketing. What will people get by reading your book that will help them solve their problem? After they finish your book, what will they be able to do or stop doing? What will change for the better in their lives?

If you are writing for therapists, promise them something they would like: *effectively dealing with the most difficult clients; engaging reluctant or passive teenagers in treatment; collecting fees easily and quickly.* Obviously, don't promise something if you can't deliver it, but your readers are usually looking for solutions. Articulate a promise on which you can deliver that matters to your target reader.

Here is a worksheet to help you get clear on the promise you are making to the readers of your book.

THE PROGRAM OR PRESCRIPTION

How-to books are sometimes called prescriptive nonfiction books. That is because they usually include some sort of system, sequence, or steps that help the reader apply the ideas in the book. In the next section, I discuss making certain your book is unique and doesn't duplicate other books in the marketplace. But here we will help you develop a unique program or prescription as one way to ensure this uniqueness.

Elizabeth Kubler-Ross was perhaps the first person to give a system for understanding and making sense of the grief process. By now, most people have come to believe that there are actually five stages of grief. But let me be very clear here: There are not five stages of grief (it is a messy process that can't really be contained in some step-by-step program).

✐   The Promise Worksheet   ✐

What will they know or be able to do or stop doing or prevent or recover from after reading your book?

When they read this book, they will know or be able to or accomplish the following:

How will this book help readers?

Hint: The promise usually taps into negative motivations (help me decrease or avoid something I don't like [e.g., anxiety, depression, getting out of a bad job]; avoid a divorce; avoid getting my book rejected by publishers) or positive motivations (help me get something I want or get more of something I want [e.g., getting rich; having peace; finding my ideal relationship; getting a book published]).

But Kubler-Ross's program was so compelling that it imposed a structure on reality and continues to do so today. Her program helped many people make sense of and get through their grief.

That is the power of a program or prescription. It helps the reader organize and make meaning of, and often use, ideas and methods to fulfill the author's promise. If you were writing a book on how to manage a borderline personality disorder diagnosis, it would help to come up with a sequence for treatment. Marsha Linehan did, and she changed the way borderline personality disorder is treated all over the world. Her dialectical behavior therapy (or DBT) is popular, as are the books and workbooks she has written based on her prescriptive model. (By the way, it is also good if your approach starts to be referred to by an acronym; if I were buying futures in diagnoses or treatment methods, I would always invest in the ones that are known by their initials).

REBT (another acronym for rational emotive behavioral therapy) has the ABCD method of challenging irrational beliefs to help people feel better and make positive changes. This makes the method easy to learn and remember.

Time frames are used as organizing principles as well. One of my editors told me that one of the first books she edited was *Lose 10 Pounds in 21 Days* and that the book was the only one of her early books still in print because that program was so compelling for diet-book buyers.

Remember the popular self-help book *The Seven Habits of Highly Effective People*? Using numbers or steps is a tried and true method of organizing a program.

The acronym is another popular way of creating a program. You could come up with the ACT program for overcoming procrastination, or the SAVE method of getting out of debt.

If you were writing a book about preventing divorce, you could fit your ideas into an acronym such as STAY. Think for a moment: What would you put into each of those categories? How about this?

S: Stop any legal actions in order to give yourself time to calm down and discover whether the divorce is really necessary.

T: Tell your partner all the reasons why you want to leave as well as all the reasons to stay. Get everything out on the table: the good, the bad, and the ugly.

A: Appreciate all the good things about your partner and the marriage and all the ways you have contributed to the problems (with no blaming the other).

Y: Yield and do not try to prove your point or be right.

Now maybe that acronym doesn't have best-seller written all over it, but come on, I just came up with it on the spot and now I have a program that no one else who is writing about preventing divorce has. It's pretty memorable too. I could organize part of my book around it, writing one chapter on each of the four aspects of the program.

Obviously, you don't want to jam your ideas into an acronym just to be memorable. I have had to discard several acronyms I came up with because fitting my ideas into them was just too tortuous or cutesy.

You could just have a sequence of ideas or methods and not any particularly memorable way of organizing them or putting them into a program. But the book would still reflect your slant on things, so don't be untrue to yourself if all these program and prescription ideas don't work for you or the book. If they do, though, they may help you get clearer and more focused and help your book be more successful.

While I wrote this book, I received an advertisement for a new book called *Fire Child, Water Child* by Stephen Scott Cowan. The subtitle is *How Understanding the Five Types of ADHD Can Help You Improve Your Child's Self-Esteem and Attention.* Cowan puts forth a scheme in which he divides attention-deficit hyperactivity disorder into five categories, each with its own element attached: Fire, Wood, Earth, Metal,

Water. Each of these types has some attributes associated with it. Again, are there really "Wood children"? No, but it is a handy way to make the complex nature of ADHD understandable and it gives parents a handle on dealing with their troubled or challenging children.

So, get creative and come up with your own scheme, initials, categories, labels, numbered lists, and so on to create your book's program. After thinking about it, what kinds of steps, sequences, or initials can you put your ideas into?

Below I have provided another worksheet for developing your prescription or program.

✐   The Prescription/Program Worksheet   ✐

My readers will get to where I've promised. They will get there by following my program or prescription, which consists of the following steps or points:

Use initials:
For example, the **FIRM** method of overcoming impotence:
   Free yourself from performance pressures.
   Investigate and rule out possible medical causes.
   Redirect your attention to your partner and to pleasure,
      rather than to performance.
   Make it mutual so neither partner gets the blame but both
      are involved in the solution.

Use numbers or time frames:
_____ steps

_____ days, weeks, months

Use alliteration:
Six Steps to Stopping Bullying in Schools

POPULATION

Next up in focusing your book is to identify clearly who your readers are likely to be. This is an area in which most authors fail. They go overboard in their population target: "Everyone can benefit from my book." Yes, perhaps (although I and your publisher are skeptical on that point).

Think about it this way. Let's imagine that you had to mail a brochure about your book to everyone in your target reader group. Imagine how much it would cost to mail that brochure to all 300 million Americans (or even more appalling, to all seven billion people in the world). That isn't realistic.

So let's start to narrow it down. How about psychotherapists? From what I can gather from research on the web, there are about 1 million English-speaking psychotherapists in the world (or course, your book might be translated, but we are trying to narrow things down, right?). That is still an expensive brochure printing and mailing job. Again, from what I can gather there seem to be about 300,000 to 400,000 psychotherapists in the United States. That is still a lot of therapists. How about therapists who practice brief therapy? Now we are getting narrower. That is perhaps 50,000 to 60,000 therapists. Woo hoo. Maybe we *can* mail out that many brochures.

The same principle applies with books for the general public. The more narrow the audience, the easier it will be to sell your book to a publisher as well as to market it to potential readers. If people outside your target population pick it up and read it, fine, but your efforts and focus will be on getting as many people in your identified market to hear about and pick up the book.

This leads into what many marketers call *niching*. Niching is finding a narrow focus for your book by finding a unique topic and a specific, targeted group of potential readers. So writing a book about stress management would not be your best initial approach, typically (unless you are Dr. Phil or Deepak Chopra, who have what publishers call a "big platform" and can probably get away with writing about any topic and find an audience). A book about stress management that is meant for accountants is a better idea.

Dealing with divorce is a topic of interest to a large potential population and has also been covered by others. What about pet custody issues in divorce? That is a smaller, more specific group and one that would be much easier to market. You could advertise or write an article for pet lovers' magazines or find bloggers or podcasters looking for guests to interview about topics for their audience of pet lovers. Or you could talk to family lawyers, mediation professionals, or collaborative divorce coaches about your book or you can write for their newsletters.

I thought about calling this book *Narrow Focus, Big Platform* (we'll get to the concept of the platform in a later chapter). These two ingredients (focus and platform) are the key to successfully selling a book to a publisher and to readers. William Zinsser, in his book *On Writing Well*, writes, "Every writing project must be reduced before you start to write it." Part of this reduction is in your book's targeted population.

On the next page I have provided a list of questions that might help you clarify and narrow your book's niche audience. Take a few minutes to answer these questions and live with them for some time before plunging on to writing your book. You will increase your chances for success if you do.

The Population Worksheet

My target audience is . . .

I want to reach everyone who . . .

The people who really need my book are . . .

The people who will most want my book are . . .

The statistics I have gathered to indicate the size (or motivation) of the potential audience for my book are . . .

Identifying Your Niche

What is or could be a focus for you?

- Some area or topic you love and are fascinated by
- Some area in which you are dissatisfied and think things could be better
- Some area in which you have accomplished something
- Some area in which you have done research and come up with some new data or findings
- Some area on which you have a new perspective or slant

Which people would be interested in this area/niche and how will you find them?

- What publications do they read?
- What other media do they consume?
- What groups or organizations do they belong to?
- What meetings or conferences do they attend?
- Who else has sold to this group or connected with them in some way?
- Who are the experts or well-known people in this area/niche?

On the following page, I have given you another worksheet to help you identify your target audience and readers.

POSITIONING

Your book has to fill a hole that is not already filled in the publishing marketplace. So, this P is about positioning your book so that it is unique and covers material that other published books haven't. You can do this either by focusing on a readership that hasn't been targeted by the information in your book (which we covered in the population section already) or by emphasizing the innovative slant and perspective you bring to the topic. Because of your expertise, you bring a credibility to the topic that others wouldn't be able to do in the same way.

This book is an example of a book that fills a unique position. There really aren't many books out there for therapists on how to write books and get published. Of the ones that are out there, none are like this one.

The reasons for this are that I am a psychotherapist who has written and published many books and I have coached many others, including many therapists, to write and publish books. Another therapist could have written a book about writing and publishing for those in our field, but few have the credibility of having so many of their own publications and to have coached many publications to completion.

In addition, I have a unique program or prescription for getting you to focus your book (the several Ps we are covering in this chapter and the last), as well as a psychological perspective on how to overcome writing blocks and procrastination.

When I teach workshops, I give away my handouts and tell participants that they are welcome to copy and use them. I also give away copies of my slides with the same permission. My former wife, who was a bit more fearful than I am about getting ripped off, expressed her concern that others could just go out and start teaching my workshops, losing business for me. I reassured her that the workshop would not be as good without me there to teach it. And, without being egotistical, I think that I have a certain power as a speaker. I have a unique and energetic style, with a lot of spontaneous humor, that no one could emulate precisely.

That is your goal for your book. You need to write a book that others could not write, even if they had similar ideas. Your voice, your unique take on the subject, your sequencing and organizing of the material are all what create your unique positioning.

If your outline or writing sample seems like something others have or could write, trash them and start over. Keep going with this process until you discover your own way of describing and seeing things. Find the hole in the market and position your book to fill in what's missing.

Take some time to fill out the Positioning Worksheet in order to ensure that you have made your book as unique as you can before you try to publish it or pitch it to an agent or publisher.

  Positioning Worksheet: Finding Your Unique Slant

How is my approach to this issue different from anything else I have seen or heard on the subject?

Other books are for anyone with this issue. Mine is targeted more narrowly to . . . (e.g., women; people about to get divorced; Southerners; parents of autistic kids having trouble getting insurance reimbursement)

No one else has my program or prescription, which is . . .

My writing or content is unique because . . . (e.g., I use cartoons or I have done a study that no one else has)

I know there are no books out there like mine because . . .

What will surprise people about my book or my approach to this topic is . . .

My unique background, credibility, accomplishments, or experience that make this a book no one else could write is . . .

THE HIGH-CONCEPT ELEVATOR SPEECH

Another way to focus your book is to work on and articulate its "high concept." A high concept is the most succinct statement of the main point of your book. The old phrase "in 25 words or less" applies here. This statement shouldn't go on and on, and you should be able to describe it in a minute or two. The high concept is sometimes called an "elevator speech." This term comes from Hollywood. Imagine you are an aspiring screenwriter and you happen to get on an elevator at the same time Steven Spielberg does. Here's your big chance to pitch your terrific screenplay. You turn to him and begin: "I have this manuscript. It's almost finished. It's kinda complicated, but you see there's this one character who comes in mid-movie that changes everything. But, wait, let me tell you about how the movie opens. It's amazing." Ding. The elevator stops at Mr. Spielberg's floor and he hastily departs with a quizzical glance back at you as the doors close.

If you only had several floors of an elevator ride to tell an agent or publisher or reader about your book, what would you say? That is your high-concept or elevator speech.

Many authors have a tough time with this. They are too close to their material and so enamored of every nuance of the idea they have that they have a hard time simplifying it in order to tell others about it.

William Zinsser, quoted earlier in this chapter, writes about this practice of articulating your book's clear focus: "Every successful piece of nonfiction should leave the reader with one provocative thought that he or she didn't have before. Not two thoughts, or five—just one."

I mentioned my book *Do One Thing Different*. When I got booked on *Oprah*, the publisher decided to put some serious effort into promoting the book and booked a 20-city radio satellite tour (this involves me doing 20 short interviews with radio stations all over the country from my home by telephone). When the paperback version came out a year after the initial hardcover release, the publisher again sprang for another 20-city radio satellite tour.

By the end of those two satellite tours, after having to say what my book was about and tell a couple of hints and stories in sometimes fewer than 5 minutes, I got very good at giving the book's high concept: It's easier to make small changes than dramatic ones. If you are unhappy with any part of your life, experiment with small changes in three areas: the Doing (actions and interactions); the Viewing (focus of attention and meanings/points of view); and the Context (the physical setting and environment around the situation). Not all of them will work, but one of them is likely to.

After I got this clear, I wished I could go back and rewrite the book. The book, in contrast to the simple, clear high concept you read above, was all over the place. I had sections on "solution-oriented spirituality," "solution-oriented sexuality," "relationship rescue," and all sorts of other things that didn't fit with that core message. I could have written a much better book that would have been easier to sell and to write if I had taken the time to develop this clarity before writing my thoughts down.

Take a lesson from that and spend some time getting your core message down to a brief statement you can make clearly and compellingly in a minute or two. The desired result should be that readers can't wait to buy your book and that editors and publishers will want to publish it.

Here's one more example. As I wrote this, I had a new book released, which was called *The Change Your Life Book*. This time, unlike with *Do One Thing Different*, I worked out my high concept *before* I did any publicity. So here is my quick high concept: *The Change Your Life Book* is designed to help you get unstuck and have a better life by engaging in fun and easy little experiments every week for one year.

I can say that in about a minute. See if you can get your high concept down to that kind of statement.

Here is a worksheet to help you create your high-concept elevator speech.

✏️ The High-Concept Elevator Speech ✏️

The shortest description I can give of my project is . . .

My book is a combination of these two well-known books or writing styles or content or well-known people or cultural or movie concepts: (e.g., Dr. Phil and Dr. Ruth; John Gray combined with Donald Trump; ET meets Sigmund Freud).

Here's one that sold in August 2005: Layne Maheu's *Crow Song*, the story of Noah's Ark told from the perspective of a crow: *Watership Down* meets *The Red Tent*.
Describe yours similarly (in the form ____meets ____; ____ in ____; ____ for _____; In the tradition of ____ but ___; reminiscent of ____ but ____; or ____ with/without ___):

If you could make a visual image of my book, it would look like this:

My book is like . . . (e.g., a soothing balm on a painful sunburn; a map to a lost traveler).

✏️ Practice Your High-Concept Statement ✏️

Choose one popular book you know fairly well and write the high-concept statement for it below:

[If you can't think of any titles, here are some possibilities: *Harry Potter and the Sorcerer's Stone*; *Men Are From Mars, Women Are From Venus*; *Getting the Love You Want*; *Seabiscuit*; *Who Moved My Cheese?*; *The Secret*; *Fifty Shades of Grey*; *The Hunger Games*.]

Investigative Research Idea: Conference Brochures

One simple way to put all the focusing ideas together is to attend a large multifaculty conference and look at the titles, descriptions, problems, promises, and potential attendees of the sessions (or get the brochure for the conference). Why I suggest you attend is that you can check out the sessions with what you think are good titles and descriptions to see whether that topic and description brought in a crowd. For this, you might exclude the well-known figures in the field, because they will probably get a good turnout, whatever the topic and description, just because they are well known. Focus instead on the little-known presenters. Notice what caught you about the title, subtitle, or description and use that to raise your awareness of these focusing elements.

FINDING A GREAT TITLE AND SUBTITLE

Sometimes the titles I came up with for my books worked and the publishers to which I sold my books stuck with my title ideas and sometimes they didn't. I remember I had what I thought was a great title for one of my books: *Insanity Is Doing the Same Thing Over and Over and Expecting Different Results*. The publisher liked the book idea but informed me in no uncertain terms that my title would not be the final one. I pushed back a little. I told them I had tried the title out on workshop audiences and they all liked it and chuckled when they heard it. It would also bring in 12-step program readers, because the saying is popular in 12-step groups.

"You can't say that title on television," they responded. "It's too long."

"I talk fast," I countered.

Still no go. The book's title ended up being *Do One Thing Different*, and due to that title, actually, the book landed me on *Oprah*. (Apparently Oprah was saying to her producers that she wanted her show to help viewers do one thing different each day, and one of her producers had my book and held it up to show her.) But it is not easy to choose a title that both publishers and readers will like.

Then a light bulb came on for me. I had studied family systems theory and also neurolinguistic programming (NLP) early in my psychotherapy career. Both of these approaches emphasized the discernment of patterns. *Why don't I just study the patterns of best-selling books?*, I thought.

Luckily for me, I found a website that listed best-selling book titles in the United States from 1900 to the present. The lists started with fiction but also listed nonfiction titles starting in 1911. So, I printed them all out and got to work. And I did discover a pattern, which I will share with you now, so that you don't have to do the research yourself!

Now, of course, you may not be aiming for the best-seller list and there is no guarantee that your book will become a best-seller (or even a good seller) if you follow this pattern, but why go against success? Why not at least adopt what people have done that works for titles and hope it helps your book? It probably won't hurt and will narrow your options as you are considering titles.

Are you ready? Here's the pattern: Best-selling book titles, with very few exceptions, are one- to four-word titles. (One of the exceptions is *Everything You Always Wanted to Know About Sex, But Were Afraid to Ask*; that doesn't count, because we all know that sex sells whatever the length of the title.) It will be even better if you can make it one or two words. *Seabiscuit. Lolita. Jaws.* Many fiction best-sellers are two words, with the first one being *The. The Shining. The Godfather. The Exorcist. The Alchemist.*

This pattern makes sense because shorter titles are easier to remember and ask for in the bookstore (remember book-stores, you older readers?) or to type into the Amazon.com search engine. I read somewhere that the original title of Napoleon Hill's *Think and Grow Rich* was *How to Use Your*

Noodle to Make a Boodle. Even though the original title was cute, the final four-word title most likely helped to make this book a perennial best-seller.

Of course, your book's subtitle can be a lot longer. You may even have several subtitles (one of my books had three subtitles; two of which were provided by the publisher). The subtitle can contain some of the detail the title may have left out, such as who the audience is. I also recommend that, in the case of nonfiction, you mention the book's problem, promise, population, and program in the title and subtitle, if at all possible.

My friend and colleague Michele Weiner-Davis practically sold her popular book *Divorce Busting* on the basis of its title alone. It is two words and carries the promise of preventing divorce with it. If I were going to create a subtitle for Michele's book, it would be something like *A Practical, Positive Program for Couples to Stay Together Even When Divorce Seems Inevitable.*

Of course, there are other aspects to titles than the number of words.

- Alliteration can be a nice way to make a catchy and memorable title: *The Happy Hooker; Possibilities for a Pain-Free Life for Parkinson's Patients; Divorce for Dummies.*
- Another title convention is to use imagery: *The Red Tent; Eye of the Needle; What Color Is Your Parachute?*
- Or you could use metaphors or metaphorical frames: *Men Are From Mars, Women Are From Venus; Chicken Soup for the Soul.*
- You could also use some variation on a well-known phrase or song lyric: *I've Come Undone; The Joy of Checks; The Gospel According to Biff; Read My Hips.*
- If you can get your target audience into the title or subtitle, all the better: *Finances for Newlyweds; Social Media Guide for the Newly Retired.*

- Another title convention is the use of opposites: *Rich Dad, Poor Dad*; *The Positive Power of Negative Thinking*.
- Create a reversal of received wisdom or advice: *Die Poor*; *Post-Traumatic Success*.
- Use a question in your title to intrigue readers: *Who Says Elephants Can't Dance?*
- Try using repetition or puns. Check out these two similar titles that used one or another of these: *Change Your Brain, Change Your Life*; *Change Your Brain and Keep the Change*.

Of course, no matter how hard you work on your title, don't get too attached to it if you are seeking a traditional publisher. Most of my books have had title changes between the time I sold them to the book publisher and the final publication.

Take some time to brainstorm your title on this worksheet, and perhaps run your ideas by friends and family to get initial reactions and feedback.

✏️   Title, Subtitle, and Topic Worksheet   ✏️

Here are three possible one- to four-word titles for my book:

This is a subtitle that contains a statement of the problem and the promise (and perhaps the program and population):

Possibilities for coming up with titles and subtitles:

Visual images

Metaphors or metaphorical frames

Variations on familiar phrases or songs or books or movie titles

The audience for the book

Opposites

Reversal of the usual expectations or received wisdom

A question

Repetition, rhyme, or puns

Numbers (4 ways to . . . ; 5 strategies . . .; the 10 steps . . .)

Time frames (. . . in 15 days or less; right away; within 6 months)

WRITE YOUR BACK COVER

Another way to get clear on your focus and content is to write the back-cover description of the book and the flap copy. Check out some book you already own (if you have any physical books around, you Kindlers and iPadders). Or visit a bookstore and check out the flaps and back covers of some books in your genre or niche.

Try emulating the pithiness and marketing savvy of those books (after all, they got published and made it to a bookstore or to your bookshelf). Notice what grabs you or grabbed you about the book. Does the copy tell you something about the author that gives him or her credibility? Is there something about the content that grabs you or that you find compelling? Are there bullet points to quickly summarize the main points or benefits (promise) of the book?

I've given you a worksheet below to guide you through this process. Take a little time and do the exercise and the worksheet. You may be surprised what emerges and how it helps you write a better book.

 Writing Back-Cover Copy

Write a brief description of your book that would grab a potential reader:

What three to six bullet points/promises/benefits would you put underneath that copy?

Write a brief biographical statement that would also be relevant to readers and grab them in some way. (This is essentially a brief "platform" statement, telling the reader why you are qualified to write this book and what your major accomplishments or "claims to fame" are.)

YOUR BOOK'S ORIGIN STORY

Some years ago, when I was a starving college student, I had a bad habit of overspending on books. I loved reading and I'm an information junkie. But this habit was wreaking havoc on my diet and health. In some weeks I would run out of money and wouldn't be able to afford food for a few days.

I was in the college bookstore one day and came across a book that intrigued me. It was about affirmations. I had read a little about affirmations, but this book claimed to have a different slant on them. I glanced through it, but prudence and the thought of my budget prevailed, and I decided to put the book back and stick to my budget. Just before I put it back on the shelf, though, I turned to the introduction and read the story of how the author had come up with this new slant.

Sondra Ray was a psychiatric nurse and lived in California. She had had a series of car accidents over the previous several years (some her fault and some not). But her insurance rate had risen so high after these accidents that she simply couldn't afford it any longer. She sold her car and relied on friends and taxis to go places that she couldn't reach by bus. This was quite inconvenient.

Some of her friends went to a lecture by a man named Leonard Orr. They came back and told Ray that they had figured out her problem while listening to the lecture. Orr contended that we all have an unconscious death wish. Ray's accidents could be explained this way, they said. Ray was skeptical, but her friends invited her to attend the next lecture Orr was giving so she could decide for herself.

She attended the lecture and was still not convinced, but she was intrigued that Orr claimed to have found a way to eliminate the death wish by using an approach to doing affirmations, which are positive statements to reprogram and eliminate negative unconscious beliefs. His method was to have a person repeat the positive affirmations (through writing or speaking) and then to respond with skepticism, doubts, negative beliefs, or any objections the mind came up with. You had to keep repeating the affirmations until no more objections arose in order to let them become more firmly established as new positive programs.

Ray went up to Orr and asked what she could do if she were skeptical and didn't believe the method would work. Orr told her he didn't think she needed to believe anything. She should try the method on something small and testable first and then use it on more serious, deeply unconscious beliefs like the death wish.

Ray went home and began to use the method, focusing on attracting dates. She had been going through a dry period with relationships and wanted to date more. Within days of starting her affirmation practice, she began to get asked out. Men she used to date called her out of the blue. Guys in coffeeshops asked her out. She was impressed and become a convert to the method. Ultimately, she got her insurance restored at a reasonable rate and never had another accident.

I went home after reading that story and the next day I came back and bought the book. The story had hooked me. This was not just another author making up some ideas and writing a book to get rich. This woman had lived this and it had worked for her.

I began to think of this kind of narrative as the book's "origin story." When and how did the author get the original idea or impulse that led to the book? When did she discover the method or slant on the topic? What was the pivotal life experience that crystallized the value or need for the approach or the book?

My first book, *Shifting Contexts*, arose from an experience I had when I was about 10 years old. I was dribbling a basketball down my long driveway and suddenly had a realization: Most of the world's trouble arose because people perceived and interpreted things differently, but they assumed that everyone else saw them the same way they did. I knew at the time this was a profound perspective, but also realized that, at 10, I didn't have the facility to articulate it in a way that would make any difference to others. I made a silent vow to myself that someday, when the time was right, I would use this insight to help others and make the world a better place. *Shifting Contexts* was about applying epistemology to psychotherapy. Epistemology is the study of how we know what we know, and it levels a skeptical eye on claims of absolute knowledge.

I never wrote that origin story to include in the book, but it was a guiding focus that helped me work out what the book's central theme was. It can be the same for you. If you can, find your book's origin story. Write it out for yourself. You might even include it in the manuscript if it is relevant, if it would help the reader know what moved you to write the book, and if it illustrates the theme in a compelling way.

The origin story is an anecdote that relates an actual or amalgamated incident that catalyzed the writing of the book. It also indicates the problem and why you are passionate about solving it. The story does not have to be about you, but you probably had a strong reaction to it.

DECIDING YOUR DIRECTION FOR PUBLICATION: SELF-PUBLISHING OR TRADITIONAL PRINT PUBLISHING?

The next chapter is on the platform, a publishing buzzword for your reputation and ability to sell books. If you decide to go with a traditional print publisher, especially for a book for the general public (called a *trade* book in the publishing industry), the platform will be a crucial element in your success or failure to secure a contract offer.

But here I want to help you get clear and focused on your pathway for publication.

Self-Publishing a Print Edition

When I first began writing, self-publishing was viewed with disdain by most people. It meant that one couldn't get a "real" publisher. Self-published books often had cheesy, poorly designed covers and were usually badly in need of editing. Those who did a good job on their self-published books faced an uphill battle to get their titles into bookstores and to get book distributors to stock them. I heard a purveyor of self-publishing, or vanity book packages, once admit that authors who hired him to print their self-published books sold an average of only 100 copies. Because their contracts usually set a minimum print run of hundreds if not thousands of copies to get the price per copy down to a reasonable one (in order to offset the cost of printing), that meant that most self-published authors had boxes of books languishing in their garages, basements, or storage units for a long, long time.

These days some of that stigma has disappeared. The thorny issue of getting distribution is also mostly a nonissue because Amazon.com allows self-published authors to easily tap into its sales and distribution system. Electronic self-publishing (or e-self-publishing) is becoming more and more common, even for traditionally published authors. It is strikingly easy to do and there is more profit in it for self-published authors than there is in self-published print versions (and, often, than there is in traditionally published print versions).

Many years ago, I decided to self-publish two books that I thought were unlikely to be published by my traditional publishers. I did end up earning more money per book, but it was a boatload of work to produce the books and ship them to people. After several years of selling them, I let them go out of print and sold one to a traditional publisher (W. W. Norton Professional Books, the publisher of this book). I heaved a sigh of relief at not having those boxes of books in my garage any longer (I had to get 5,000 printed at a time to get the best price. It took me several years to sell all those books). When Norton bought the copyright, they did change a few things, which irritated me, but I decided not to fight about them. The original self-published book had a few raunchy jokes in it and my editor at Norton thought they were inappropriate for a professional book, so she asked me to edit them out. The back cover of the original self-published book had fake endorsements such as "I couldn't put it down."—Venus de Milo; and "It rolls up into a cylinder."—Sigmund Freud. I thought these were hilarious (so did some of my readers) and I would change them for each printing. But the fake blurbs had to go. Still, Norton kept some of the quirky elements (whimsical little illustrations on many of the pages, and some psychotherapist jokes in the back of the book), so I guess I shouldn't complain too much. I tell you this story to emphasize that when you let others publish your books, you are entering into a relationship, and like all relationships, this involves some compromises. You cede control, but you often end up with less work and a more professional product.

The reasons for why most self-published books don't do well are the following:

1. They are poorly conceived, without the proper focus and audience in mind.
2. They are poorly written, not well edited, and not well designed (both their interiors and their covers).
3. They aren't distributed or marketed well.

If you can overcome these typical problems and are willing to seek out a professional editor and designer to help you make the book look good and read well, self-publishing may be for you.

Reasons for why you might want to self-publish or e-self-publish:

1. Relatively rapid time to publication. A traditional print book might take 1 to 2 years from conception to print publication. A self-published book can be on the market within months.
2. More profit per book. While it is often more work producing a self-published book and you might have to invest some money upfront, your earnings per book will almost certainly be higher than if you sold your book to a traditional publisher.
3. More control over all aspects of the book. You get to choose the cover design, the interior design, the book price, the release date, and the cover copy. You also continue to own the rights in perpetuity. You can always re-edit it and put out a new version.
4. The book never has to go out of print. Most traditionally published print books have a limited shelf life and will go out of print. Because you have no corporate offices to maintain, shareholders to answer to, or large amounts of money invested that needs to earn a return, you can afford to keep your book in print forever.

Having said all that, self-publishing, though much easier and more affordable these days, is still a lot of work. You either have to do that work yourself by putting in a lot of time and learning things that are not easy for most of us, or you have to hire someone to do it for you.

Self-Publishing E-books

E-publishing is a lot easier than print publishing. Little or no money needs to be invested upfront. There is no need to store copies in your garage or basement. Amazon.com and the Apple iStore will let you put your e-books on their sites for free; they will also sell them for you and send you your share of the profits. So, e-self-publishing has many of the advantages of self-publishing (control, rapid time to publication, retained owner-ship, always in print, etc.) with fewer drawbacks or challenges.

Amazon.com announced in May 2011 that it was selling more e-books than print books. I never thought I would be an e-book reader. I treasured print books as sacred objects. As a teen, if I read a paperback book, I would be careful not to crack the spine because I wanted the book to remain pristine. I amassed a collection of about 8,000 books over the years.

But a number of moves and a lack of space (plus a vindic-tive ex-spouse who "accidentally" let my books get soaked in a rainstorm before I could find a place for them) led me to radically downsize my library.

I was traveling overseas to some non-English-speaking coun-tries several years ago and ran out of books to read on the long first flight. I was desperate for reading material that whole trip (I read several books a week). When I returned home, Amazon emailed me, offering to give me a free trial of their just-released Kindle e-book reader. I was skeptical, but, remembering the frustration of not having books with me on my travels and with Amazon's guarantee of a refund not only for the Kindle itself, but for any e-books I bought during the trial period, I decided to give it a try. Fast-forward three years and I am now hooked on e-books. I like that they don't clutter up my space (formerly a pack rat, I am trying to go Zen simple and clear out my phys-ical surroundings as the years go on and before the TV show *Hoarders* shows up on my doorstep). I like that I can carry thou-sands of books with me at a time on a small device that takes up little room in my carry-on bag (I read on my iPad these days by using the Kindle or iBooks apps). I love that I can instantly look up words in the dictionary. I can turn down pages, highlight sections, make notes associated with sections of the text, and search within them and print them out later. I have the book forever and don't have to store it anywhere but in cyberspace. I am an e-book convert. I rarely buy a physical book anymore. My future mother-in-law, at 92, couldn't get out of the house to feed her book-a-day habit and is now also hooked on the Kindle app on her iPad. She never runs out of books either. She can reset the type size of the book to be larger as her vision deteriorates. We can lend each other books electronically. If she and I have converted, I think e-books are the future.

Getting your e-book onto the distribution channels for e-books is relatively easy, even for nontechnical people, and it is free or very low cost, but you can also hire services to do the technical bits for you.

E-book Publishing Services

Here is a quick guide to the major e-book self-publishing services if you decide to go this route. Be aware that things in cyberspace change rapidly (the old joke was that each month of the web's development was measured in dog years), so this information may be different when you act on it.

The 800-pound gorilla in the e-book publishing and distribution space is Amazon.com's Kindle Desktop Publishing (https://kdp.amazon.com/). Start with them (unless you go with Book-Baby, which has the ability to get your books on the Kindle platform).

The other three I would recommend are the following:

- BookBaby.com (charges a small fee for getting your book ready in the e-book format and distribution; takes a percentage of the profit; will add more services such as editing and cover design for more money).
- Smashwords.com (costs nothing to host your e-books and distribute them; takes a percentage of the sales on each book).
- Apple.com's iBookstore (costs nothing to get your e-books into their publishing and distribution channel; takes a percentage of your sales as its fee; also has the capacity to let you host and create multimedia versions of your e-books with embedded audio and video clips).

There is a lot more to know about publishing e-books and, as I mentioned, the world of e-books is changing so rapidly that I recommend that you buy a more specialized book about the subject or get some training if you decide this is the direction you would like to take.

Traditional Print Publishing

Most of the books I have written have been produced by traditional print publishers. Going this route is a bit harder because publishers have to be more selective about which books they publish: each title requires an investment of time, attention, and money, and there is a greater need to make a profit.

Whenever I told people over the years that I wrote books, they would often ask me who had published my books. When I mentioned W. W. Norton, HarperCollins, John Wiley and Sons, Penguin, and other big New York-based publishers, I would usually hear, "Oh, you're a real writer then." Many people see traditional publishers as those who legitimatize the authors.

Traditional print publishers generally fall into two categories: smaller, professional, specialized, or university presses, and the large New York-based publishers. Books for the general public are trade books. Right now, you are reading a professional book, written and targeted to psychotherapists. The latter type of book is easier to get published (not easy, just easier).

To get a trade book published, because the market is so competitive (and the upfront money and potential income is usually larger than other books), you usually need a literary agent to represent you and pitch your book. Larger trade publishers are so overwhelmed by the number of people who want to submit book projects to them that they have farmed out the filtering of these projects to agents. The agents only pass on the most promising projects to the acquiring editors and their assistants.

That means that finding an agent to represent your book can be challenging. Agents only want to pitch projects that are likely to sell. They work on commission, so they don't want to pitch too many unlikely projects to editors at publishing houses or sell too many that don't make a profit, because then editors will be less likely to consider future pitches.

When you self-publish or e-self-publish, you need to write the whole book upfront, but with traditional print publishers, you only need to write several sample chapters and a proposal describing what the book will be about along with your plans to market and sell it to (potentially) get a contract. So, even though it may seem counterintuitive, you sell your book before you write it in this situation (however, if you are writing novels, memoirs, or poetry, this does not hold and you will have to write all or a substantial portion of the book before you get a contract).

If you decide to go with a traditional publisher, you will need to prepare a book proposal and I'll cover that in the next chapter. You will also need to work on building your audience and marketing abilities, and I'll cover that in the chapter about your platform. In addition to the focusing work discussed in this chapter, the elements that will determine whether or not you succeed in getting a contract to write a traditionally published print book are having a well-prepared proposal and a well-developed platform.

The bar is very high for getting a contract and an advance from a large New York publisher through an agent. Your platform and proposal have to be extremely compelling. For smaller presses, the bar isn't so high; if you have a good proposal, a unique and well-thought-out and focused book idea, and a decent platform, you are likely to succeed in getting a contract.

What are the benefits of going this route? These publishers will create professionally produced books that other people format, edit, design, and distribute. I have become a much better writer for having been edited and guided by tradi-tional editors. Also, I have made a good amount of money, both upfront and in ongoing royalty payments, that should continue into my retirement and even after my death to help support my family.

Traditional print publishers and agents also have better contacts with foreign book publishers, making it easier to arrange for translations of your work and to track and administer the payments for those translated copies. My books have been translated into 16 different languages, mostly due to the efforts of my publishers and agents.

You need an agent when you want a trade book contract with a big New York publishing house (or the equivalent in whatever country you live—London for the United Kingdom; Sydney for Australia). How do you get an agent to say yes?

THE FIVE ELEMENTS THAT WILL MAKE EDITORS AND AGENTS SAY YES TO YOUR BOOK PROJECT

Your Passion: Are you writing the book just for wealth or fame, or are you firmly, deeply, and passionately convinced that this book needs to exist? Have you communicated that passion without being obnoxious?

Your Platform: Is there an audience for the book as demonstrated by trends, statistics, or previous books that are different but similar to yours? Do you have a reputation as an expert? Are you well known? Can you get the word out about the book when it comes out? Are you able and willing and planning to supplement the publisher's promotional efforts? And have you communicated that to the editor or agent effectively and credibly?

Your Clear, Unique Focus: Do you have a clear and narrow-enough focus so that your book can be distinguished from others in your area? Is it clear who the potential readers are? Is your take on the topic unique? Do you have a title, subtitle, and clear problem, promise, and program statement that reflects this clear, unique focus?

Your Engaging Writing Sample: Is the writing sample you will submit compelling and engaging? Does it grab the reader emotionally?

Your Proposal: Does your proposal reflect and represent these elements well?

Approach an agent by submitting a query letter. You can query multiple agents at one time as long as you mention this in your query letter. You may wait a long time for a response or you may get a quick response with a "yes, send me your proposal" (or manuscript if you are pitching a memoir or fiction book) or a "no, thanks." If you get a no, quickly query another agent in order to keep your momentum going and to not get too discouraged. You are searching for an agent who "gets" your book and who thinks you could write and sell it. You may have to search for quite a while.

Once you get a positive response, send in your proposal. From there, the agent will either agree to represent you or not. If he or she does agree, there should be some sort of written agreement between you and the agent spelling out the terms. It's a little like lining up a real estate agent. Your agent takes a percentage of your income from the book, from the advance on until the book stops making money (even after one or both of you die). If the agent has represented your book to a publisher and it sells, the agent is usually entitled to a percentage of the royalties (usually 15%), even if he or she is no longer your agent. Again, this is a bit like a real estate agent. If you had an agent with whom you listed your house but it didn't sell, that agent would still be entitled to a commission if the house sold later to someone to whom they had shown it.

Usually these agreements can be dissolved by mutual agreement with written notice. Read your agreement thoroughly or run it by a lawyer before you sign it.

Essential Elements of Query Letters

Query letters are the usual ways in which writers get editors, publishers, and agents to consider looking at or buying nonfiction books. Writing query letters is sometimes more challenging than writing a book. As in Pascal's note to a friend, "I am sorry for the length of my letter. I had not the time to write a short one," it can be difficult to boil your 250-page book and your credentials for writing it down to one page or so. And brief is better than long even if you fear you are leaving out some of the nuances of your project. Agents and editors are usually very busy: The longer your "pitch" is, the less likely it will be read and the more likely it will be read too quickly.

Even if you have some personal connection with or have been solicited by an agent or editor, it might still be worthwhile to come up with a query letter, because your editor or agent can use a brief summary of your project in order to sell it to others. The more you can pre-think this condensed summary, the easier it will be for you to describe it to people later on when you publicize it (and perhaps it will even help you write it because you will have a much clearer idea of the focus and essence of the book).

So, even though this query letter will be short, you may spend a long time planning, preparing, and writing it, and going over it to edit for clarity and brevity. And, of course, it is essential to proofread over and over to ensure that there is not a single typo or grammatical error.

What follows is a brief structure or formula for the elements to be included in your query letter. Obviously, you will imbue the letter with your own style, but make sure you have included these important elements or your book may be rejected for reasons not having to do with its quality or content.

The 6 Ps for a Powerful Query Letter

In coaching people to get their books written and published, I have come up with a succinct formula for what should be covered in your query letter. I call it the 6P Method. Here are those 6 Ps, as succinctly as I can put them.

Particular agent/publisher: Why are you contacting this particular agent or editor with this project? Did another of their authors recommend him or her? Has the editor worked on books that are similar to yours? Are you looking for representation on just this project or do you have more projects in mind for the future?

Acquaint yourself with the agent's or editor's work before you write this section. This moves the letter from a more generic letter to a more personal one. Obviously, use the agent's or editor's name rather than addressing it to: *Dear Agent* or *Dear Editor* or *To Whom It May Concern*. It is fairly easy these days to find good information about agents and editors on the Internet these days. Or visit your local library or bookstore and look the agent or editor up in one of the reference books (my favorite is Jeff Herman's *Guide to Literary Agents, Editors, and Publishers*—it's updated every year and contains lots of personal information about agents' and editors' tastes and about other books they have represented or published). In any case, however you do it, do some homework.

Position: How does this book occupy a unique position in the market (i.e., it fills an unfilled niche; its angle or slant is unique). Also, why are you the right person for the project? Is it due to your credentials and your expertise?

Your job here is to convince the agent or the editor (and later the publishing committee) that this book is absolutely unique and fills a hole in the market. If you can't make this case, you might want to rethink the focus of the book before sending the query letter.

As I have spelled out in this chapter, uniqueness derives from several ingredients: a particular population of readers different from the specific population for other books on this subject; your unique slant or approach to the topic; and your qualifications or expertise (or fame) that makes you the right person to write this book at this time; the time is ripe for this book (be careful with this one, because it will likely be several years before the book comes out).

Population: Who, specifically, would be the likely readers of your book? It can't be everybody. If the book can be more narrowly targeted to a certain definable audience, who is that? Would it be fans of John Gray's work; middle-aged women; people on the verge of divorce? A narrowly defined audience helps sell the book and makes it more easily marketable.

This element was mentioned in the section on *Position*, but it is so important, we should discuss it a bit more in detail here. Many books fail to get the attention of an agent or an editor because the author hasn't thought through this aspect. I tell people that the entryway to first getting published (until you establish a track record of success) is through the narrow gate. Once you're Deepak Chopra, you can write about almost anything and it will get published. But you're not Deepak, so narrow it down. The more specific the audience, the easier it is to market the book to readers and the easier it is to sell it to publishers (unless it is excessively narrow, of course—it's got to be more than just hundreds of people).

Person: Who are you? Why are you passionate about and committed to this book? How did you come to know that it should be written? Why are you the right author for it?

It may be hard to communicate your passion and style in a few paragraphs, but it can be accomplished. I sometimes tell a brief "origin story" about how and why the book was conceived and why it is so important to me to write it. Again, spend some time getting your unique sensibility and voice to come through in the letter. After all, you are applying for the position of "book author" and you can show some of your qualifications if the writing is compelling and engaging.

Platform: This is a combination of three elements:

- *Portfolio:* What work have you done that gives you credibility and will impress others, especially agents and editors? You are going to send supporting materials with your proposal, but here just give a quick summary of your

literary or other accomplishments that are relevant to
writing the book or being an expert in the topic area.

- *Prestige:* How well known are you? How motivated are
your fans to buy your work? Would famous people be
willing to endorse you or give you blurbs? Have you
won awards in your field of expertise? Do you already
have blurbs or endorsements from well-known people?
Mention these in your letter and anything else that shows
your prestige. Don't be arrogant and braggy, but don't
hide your light under a bushel basket either.
- *Promotional abilities and channels:* How many people can
you inform about the book in the shortest time or over a
longer period of time? Do you have a newsletter, popular
blog, podcast, website with a lot of unique visitors per
month, or email list? Do you have a radio or TV show?
Do you have access to mass media on a regular basis?
Are you an enthusiastic, media-savvy person who can
promote your book? Do you have media training? Can
you speak in sound bites? Do bookstore owners like your
work based on your previous writing? Do you regularly
do public speaking? Do you get big audiences for those
talks?

I know I have given quite a long list above, so you may
have to pick and choose, because again you are trying to
keep the query letter to one page. Choose the most impressive or potentially biggest publicity channels or abilities and
highlight those.

Project: What genre is the book (e.g., nonfiction self-
help; chick lit; suspense; financial how-to)? What is the most
succinct summary you can give of the project? This should be
a summary of all the information above.

Again, this is sort of an "elevator speech." Imagine that
you are riding five floors in an elevator. Could your letter be
read and absorbed in this time period? If not, keep working

on it. Delete anything that is unnecessary or unclear. Keep it short, sweet, and densely packed with relevant information. You'll get a chance to stretch out and add details and nuance in the proposal, but resist the invitation to say everything about it in this letter. This is the preview of coming attractions for your book and your proposal. It's a sample of the savory meal to come, not the meal.

Responses From Agents (or Not): What Then?

If you keep getting no response from agents you have queried, keep working on your query letter or on your platform (see Chapter 5). Resubmit your revised letter to these agents, or try submitting to a different set.

If you get a positive response to your query letter but an agent turns you down after seeing your proposal, you will need to write a better proposal (and continue to work on expanding your platform) for the next agent.

Querying Publishers Directly

If you are seeking a smaller or professional publisher, you often don't need an agent. You can approach an editor at that publishing house directly with a query letter. An editor will, again, either ignore you, send you a polite rejection letter (via email usually), or ask to see your proposal. If the editor likes your proposal, he or she will offer you a contract and sometimes an advance on royalties. Again, read your contract carefully and run it by a lawyer before signing. Publishing contracts can be quite complex and, like any agreement or legal contract, can be subject to negotiation, so don't just sign away your rights or livelihood. Ask questions and negotiate.

The middle man (an agent) is missing from this equation and you get to keep all the advance and royalties in this case.

With the advent of the web and e-books, things are changing fast in the world of publishing, but most authors still hope for a traditional print publishing contract, falling back to Plan B (self-publishing and/or e-book-publishing) if that doesn't happen. I do a mixture of all three these days and they all have something to recommend them.

Okay, here is a checklist to help you stay on track with the initial steps you need to take to start on your writing and publishing journey.

ESSENTIAL STEPS TO WRITING AND PUBLISHING A BOOK

- Identify the strong passion that drives, pulls, or calls you to do this book.
- Get clear about your focused niche audience.
- Articulate a problem your book will solve for that niche audience.
- Articulate the unique slant, solution, and promise for that problem your book will offer.
- Create a working title and subtitle for your book.
- Create your brief elevator speech (include the title and subtitle, who the book is for, what problem it solves, and its unique slant, promise, and program if it doesn't make the pitch too long or unwieldy).
- Articulate your book's origin story.
- Decide preliminarily whether you will e-self-publish, self-publish in print, or seek a traditional publisher.
- Query an editor or agent and ask if he or she would be willing to look at your book proposal (more on proposals in the next chapter).
- Persist until you find an agent or publishing house that agrees to give you a contract, but be careful to read that contract and get legal advice beforehand.

CHAPTER 3

The Proposal
Never Write a Book Before You Sell It

WHEN I BEGAN WRITING BOOKS, all I had to do to get a book contract, because I had met the publisher and it was a small professional psychotherapy press, was to write a short outline and brief letter describing the book project.

When I began to branch out beyond writing for a professional audience and tried my hand at trade book publishing, I got an agent who insisted I write an extensive proposal for the publisher. I dutifully began, after having read a book about preparing proposals.

After I had written the proposal, the agent had some comments and edits and I revised it. After the revision, he had some more comments and more edits. Long story short, I worked on that proposal for three months and went through many drafts.

Frankly, I resented the process. It took me as long to write and work on that proposal as it would have to write about a third of the book it was representing. But the agent convinced me that it was a necessary effort. Editors at big publishing houses are too busy to read entire books and before they put time, money, and effort into a book, they want to see the briefer summary and business plan. They also have to present a book they want to acquire to their publishing house colleagues (their marketing and sales staff, their boss, etc.) and having a proposal helps them to "sell" the book internally.

Because I wanted to publish more trade books, I worked hard to learn how to create a compelling proposal, but for years it always seemed like a bit of a distraction to what I really wanted to do, which was just to write the book.

Professional publishers and small presses also began asking for proposals around that time, so I wrote more and more proposals as time went on (I still do a mix of professional and trade books). At some point, I realized that writing the proposal wasn't unnecessary extra work, but it actually helped me plan the book and think about it (and my marketing plans) more clearly. As I mentioned in the last chapter, having clarity up front makes for a better and more saleable book.

Creating a really well-thought-out proposal makes the book easier and faster to write. I went from taking three years to write a book to one year and eventually to being able to write books in months or weeks. The more I thought hard about the book before I wrote it, got the high concept clear, and wrote a good chapter outline, the quicker I could then write the book.

So now I recommend that even self-published authors take the time to write a proposal for their books. That is why I have included this chapter, even though some of you have already decided you will self-publish.

A proposal is like a blueprint for a house you plan to build. You can brainstorm and make changes in the design, all before you build the house and have to make expensive changes in the process of construction. Anyone who has ever built a house knows that on-the-fly changes cause problems and cost overruns. A proposal is also like a business plan because you are pre-thinking and planning how you are going to get the word about the book out and sell as many copies as it deserves.

So, how do you go about creating a proposal?

ELEMENTS OF A COMPELLING, COMPLETE PROPOSAL

Here, as succinctly as I can make it, are the typical elements included in a proposal for a nonfiction book. There is no actual required or standard form for proposals and you can be as creative as you would like, but you should have a pretty good reason to deviate from the elements listed here.

1. Title Page
2. Overview and Summary of the Book
3. Info About You, the Author
4. Manuscript Specifications
5. Chapter Summaries
6. Analysis of the Market and the Competitive Titles
7. Platform Statement/Marketing Plan
8. Sample Writing

Let's take each of these in turn.

1. Title Page

This is the cover page for the proposal. I always start with the word *Proposal* in the upper left-hand corner of the cover page. Below that, centered, should be the title and subtitle, followed by your name. If you have an agent, put his or her name and contact information below the title and subtitle. If you don't have an agent, put your own name and contact information in this area. This is all the information that should appear on this page.

2. Overview and Summary of the Book

Try to keep this as short as possible: an ideal length is two pages (double-spaced) if you can. Include more if you have to, but it's better to keep it less if you can and still get the point across.

Answer these major questions quickly and broadly (think big picture):

- What is this book: self-help; how-to; part memoir, part educational; and so on?
- Who are you and why are you the right person to write this book?
- What is the unique slant or angle of the book, who is the intended audience (and how large would that readership be) and why is the book needed by those readers?
- How will you help sell the book and get the word out about it?
- Why have you sent it to this particular agent or editor (if this is relevant)?

3. Info About You, the Author

Include a short biographical statement establishing your credibility, your credentials, your accomplishments, and your marketing channels. Keep this to a paragraph or two. You will expand on some of these areas in other sections of the proposal, so this is just a quick overview.

4. Manuscript Specifications

Write another short paragraph telling the agent or editor how long (in word count or number of pages) the book will be; whether it will have illustrations and how those will be created or obtained; if any copyright permissions or fees will be necessary to use other people's material (hint: unless it is essential for the book or you will be willing to pay, the higher these costs, the more potential strikes against the project); and the expected time you will take to deliver the manuscript (hint: this is anywhere from 9 to 18 months typically; I usually say a year).

5. Chapter Summaries

This is an expanded outline, with bullet points or short narrative summaries of what each chapter will contain. Again, this should be as short as it can be to get the point across.

6. Analysis of the Market and the Competitive Titles

This section should contain any numbers you have about the size of the potential readership for the book. And it should mention other books that are similar to yours and define how yours is different and fills a unique niche or need. I do this research by going on Amazon.com and reading reviews of related books. I also get a copy of *Books in Print* and I visit the bookstore and look at the relevant subject-area section to see if there is anything I have missed. In these discussions, don't dismiss the other books. Factually summarize them and then demonstrate how yours is different.

Hint: Don't claim that your book is entirely unique and has no competition. This may make the agent or publisher nervous, because it may indicate there is not really a market for your kind of book.

7. Platform Statement/Marketing Plan

Platform is the jargon word in the publishing industry, and it basically means anything that helps you or your book stand out from the crowd and be more likely to sell. It includes your marketing channels, your marketing capabilities, your credibility, and the size of your potential readership. (We'll discuss the platform in detail in the next chapter, so you should read that chapter before preparing this section of your proposal.)

Expand on your biographical statement by providing as much evidence as possible that the book will sell and how you can help it sell. See my proposal example below for my platform statement. I often call it "Special Marketing Opportunities and Plans" or something similar. Don't use the word "platform" or they might think you're trying too hard to be an insider (and the jargon or buzzword could change at any time).

8. Sample Writing

This consists of samples from any chapter (it doesn't matter if it is from the middle of the book) or chapters that will give the agent, editor, or publishing committee a sense of the style of the book and your writing abilities. If there will be charts, quizzes, illustrations, summary boxes, or any other special formatting, include sections in which these occur.

That's how to create a good proposal. Now let's talk about, as TV chef Emeril says, kicking it up a notch to make it more compelling.

MAKING A KICK-ASS PROPOSAL

No typos. Run spell check, and ask friends who are literate and know grammar and spelling to go over and over it. While the proposal doesn't have to be perfect, any minor errors of this kind are a turnoff and could put you in the circular file. If you have the wherewithal and are going for a trade book contract and an agent, you might want to hire a professional editor who is familiar with proposals to go over it for you.

Always double-space everything. This one drives me crazy sometimes because it seems like such a waste of paper, but this is the form editors like to see, because I guess they are used to editing and making comments on double-spaced manuscripts. In any case, I have gotten proposals kicked back to me by my agent when I have tried to sneak in a section that is single-spaced.

Include some supporting documents or media material to illustrate your platform. I have put together a packet of audiotaped excerpts of radio interviews I have done, clips from television appearances I have made, my workshop schedule for the next year or two, and newspaper and magazine articles in which my work has been featured. I send these with my proposal to add weight to it.

Print it on a high-quality printer on standard white paper with a standard font. It's always safest to use Times New Roman in 12-point size.

THINGS THAT ARE LIKELY TO LOSE YOU THE SALE

1. Not having a unique and focused approach to your topic.
2. Not having a good platform. These days, editors and agents need to make a business case for the book, no matter how great the idea or writing may be.
3. Bragging or making grandiose promises ("This is sure to be a best-seller"; "I know Oprah will want to feature me on her show").
4. Using cheesy graphics or tricks (printing the whole proposal on waxed paper; sending the proposal soaked in perfume; printing the proposal in different colored inks; using too many different fonts, and so on). It should look like a professional business document. Don't get cute.

5. Not including a self-addressed, stamped return envelope (with the right amount of postage, please). If you don't, an agent or editor might not even look at your proposal and will just recycle it. Some agents and editors are taking email submissions, so this is not relevant in that situation, but don't include your proposal attachment until you get their permission to send it (would you open an email with an attachment from someone you didn't know?).

Sample Proposal

What follows is a sample proposal to give you a sense of what the whole thing looks like. This is an actual proposal that my agent sold to a major New York publisher. It isn't perfect. I continue to learn more each time I write and sell one (or don't sell one) and as I coach others to write theirs and see what sells (and doesn't sell). But it is pretty good and certainly good enough to have secured tens of thousands of dollars as an advance. So you can use this proposal as a model. Adapt your book and platform to this format.

THE ONLY WAY OUT IS THROUGH:
Five Pathways to Power and Possibilities in Overwhelming Crisis

[Final Title: THRIVING THROUGH CRISIS: Turning tragedy and trauma into growth and change]
by Bill O'Hanlon
[I deleted my agent's name, so she doesn't get inundated with all my readers' queries.]
Your name and contact information here [*unless you have an agent, then put his or her name and contact information here*]

Overview

I came to write this book because I have had two major crises
in my life. These led to breakdowns of sorts. Not the kind
where you go into the hospital and get on psychiatric drugs.
More like the kind where I couldn't go on with my life as
I had before. My usual ways of coping or living would no
longer serve. I felt overwhelmed and devastated. The last
breakdown occurred only a few years ago so it is still all too
fresh in my memory. Although devastating at the time, both
breakdowns ultimately led to positive changes in my life. I
began to entertain the notion that crises, while painful and
potentially destructive, may have some value to them. Having
a breakdown is a bit like shooting the rapids or surfing a big
wave: There are choice points before, during, and after crises
that minimize or maximize the potential for either damage or
benefits to derive from them. The problem with breakdowns is
that people don't know how to get the benefits from them, in
part because they see them as only negative and harmful and
in part because no one ever clued them into the possibility of
possible benefits. Many people can, in retrospect, recognize the
value and growth that resulted from major crises, but this book
suggests there is a way to be more mindful of those benefits
and choice points before, during, and after the process.

I have seen many people go through crises in my 28 years
as a therapist. Some had positive outcomes and some didn't.
Sometimes crises left people broken and diminished. But other
times, just as had been the case for me, people seemed to grow,
thrive, and make positive changes in the wake of these major
crises. I began to wonder what made the difference between the
two outcomes. I wondered: *Why do people have crises and do*

they serve any useful purpose in people's lives? Are crises an inevitable part of life? If they do serve useful purposes or are inevitable, how does one maximize their usefulness and minimize their damage?

One of the differences I noticed was that some people used the crisis as an opportunity to make changes that would be too difficult in the normal course of life. Some crises occur through no fault or actions of the people involved. A loved one dies unexpectedly or tragically, financial disasters strike, one suffers a major health scare or incident, and so on. Sometimes things don't have any bigger meaning or purpose—one just gets cancer. Or one is involved in a horrible car accident or is the victim of a crime. People die. Lives are shattered. But even then, crises can be openings. During overwhelming crises, our usual coping mechanisms and taken-for-granted ways of living, are, for a time, in flux. This can create a rare opportunity to make major, and often long-overdue, changes in our lives. If we can heed the wakeup call, we can move more rapidly to the next place we are heading or we come back to ourselves and rediscover or uncover the lives we are meant to lead.

Other times, the crises are not so random. People seem to unconsciously set themselves up for breakdowns. It is as if they know at some level the lives they are leading are unworkable and they need the impetus of a major breakdown to make the necessary, but difficult, changes they need to make. They overwork or overfunction to such an extent that they have a health crisis or just collapse from fatigue. They have affairs and leave clues to their discovery. They spend money without attending to their financial means and became mired in too much debt or unmanageable back taxes. They avoid confronting problems or making needed changes. They up their prescriptions of Prozac, drink more alcohol, or read more self-help books. They try to make small adjustments rather than the major life change that is needed. This is like rearranging the deck chairs on the *Titanic*. But, no matter what they try, they can't really tap dance fast enough to avoid the crisis.

Crises may be a normal, expectable part of life. They seem to function like forest fires, clearing out the undergrowth and making room for new growth.

This is a book about how to recognize the value of crises and how to use them as opportunities for major change, renewal, and growth. As counterculture business consultant Paul Hawken has said, "Problems are opportunities in drag." Or here's the poet Rilke: *Winning does not tempt that man. This is how he grows: by being defeated decisively by constantly greater beings.*

When a major crisis happens, then, there is a possibility of two valuable things emerging from it:

One will be confronted with issues one never wanted to
    face and have a chance to resolve them;
The crisis can push people to make major changes in their
    lives that were often long overdue, but too scary or hard
    to make in the course of everyday life.

There is some evidence from social science that crises and tragedies can have positive benefits. The psychiatrist Kazimierz Dabrowski first posited a theory of "positive disintegration" in 1964 (Dabrowski, K., *Positive Disintegration* [Boston: Little, Brown & Co.]), suggesting that overwhelming crises are necessary and natural elements that help people move from one developmental stage to the next. There is even a scale that has been developed to measure perceived benefits of negative events (McMillen, J. Curtis, and Fisher, Rachel H., "The perceived benefits scales: Measuring perceived positive life changes after negative events," *Social Work Research*, September 1998, 22[3]: pp. 173–187). A wide range of positive life changes have been reported in many studies of positive effects from tragedies such as heart attacks, cancer, fires, death of loved ones, chronic illness, rape, and natural disasters. Those positive changes that have been documented are enhanced closeness with others, including loved ones and neighbors, changed life priorities, enhanced sense of self-effectiveness, enhanced sensitivity, increased knowledge about the negative event experienced (in one study, heart attack survivors were less likely to have had another heart attack and more likely to be in good health eight years post-attack if they had perceived benefit a few weeks following the attack (Affleck et al, "Causal attribution, perceived benefits, and morbidity following a heart attack," *Journal of Consulting and Clinical Psychology*, 1987, 55: pp. 29–35).

Many stories in the wake of the 9/11 terrorist attacks show that people have used that crisis as a wakeup call. In a survey taken by *USA Today* in August 2001, then again in October 2001, respondents said initially that work was their top priority, family was third. In October, family had moved up to first. Liz Rosenberg, Madonna's publicist, cited 9/11 as a major factor in her deciding to quit as Madonna's publicist because all Madonna needed in her current career was shielding from the press and that wasn't significant enough for Rosenberg. She felt that, although she was well paid, the work wasn't important enough to spend the rest of her life doing it.

The Only Way Out Is Through, then, is a roadmap for how to recover from breakdowns and crises and to reconnect with a life of meaning, passion, and aliveness. It will also give readers a way to understand and deal with what is happening during crises so they don't get stuck in them. Winston Churchill proclaimed: *When you're going through Hell, don't stop! The Only Way Out Is Through* will help readers be less afraid of the changes that crises and breakdowns bring and derive the maximum benefit from the rare opportunity that crises can provide.

About the Author

Bill O'Hanlon, M.S., L.M.F.T., has authored or coauthored 18 books, including *Do One Thing Different*, as well as numerous articles, book chapters, audiotapes, and videotapes. He has appeared on *The Oprah Winfrey Show*, *The Today Show*, and a variety of other national television programs, and his books have been translated into nine languages. Since 1977, Bill has taught over 950 seminars around the world on psychotherapy, spirituality, and relationships. Bill is a Licensed Mental Health Professional, Certified Professional Counselor, and a Licensed Marriage and Family Therapist. He lives in Santa Fe, New Mexico.

Manuscript Specifications

Around 250 pages. It can be delivered within 8 to 10 months from contract signing. The author has written or cowritten 18 previous books and has always met his deadlines. Permissions for a few poems will need to be obtained, but the author will keep these to a minimum.

Special Marketing Opportunities About Bill O'Hanlon, M.S., LMFT, CPC, LMHP

- Author or coauthor of 18 books and 42 articles and book chapters
- Produced or coproduced six audiotapes, two computer programs, and five videotapes
- Regular foreign translations of many previous books (translated into French, Spanish, Portuguese, Swedish, Finnish, German, Chinese, Bulgarian, Turkish, and Japanese)
- Extensive public speaking experience. Taught over 950 seminars in the U.S., Australia, New Zealand, Hong Kong, Japan, Scandinavia, Europe, South America, Canada, and Mexico, currently averaging four seminars a month with an average of 200 participants per seminar. Major faculty member or keynote presenter at four or five national conferences per year with thousands of attendees at each.
- Developed a method of psychotherapy called brief solution-oriented therapy, an approach that is sweeping the therapy field
- Appeared on the *Today Show*, *Oprah Winfrey Show* (as only and featured expert for the hour), Canada AM, and many other radio and TV shows
- Did two 10-city live publicity tours for previous books (*Love Is a Verb*, Norton, 1995; *Do One Thing Different*, Morrow, 1999); has done three radio satellite tours
- Has had media coaching

- Previous trade book was a selection for *Book of the Month Club*, *Quality Paperback Book Club*, and *One Spirit Book Club* ($15,000 advance)
- Previous books were endorsed by Bernie Siegel, M.D. (author of *Love, Medicine and Miracles*), Lonnie Barbach, Ph.D. (author of *For Yourself*), Ellen Kreidman, Ph.D. (author of *Light His Fire*), and Michele Weiner-Davis, M.S.W. (author of *Divorce Busting*)
- Previous trade book was excerpted in *Ladies' Home Journal* (January 2000); work has been featured in *Newsweek*, *Self*, *New Woman*, *Bottom Line*, and other national magazines
- Has a website (www.brieftherapy.com) with 20,000+ hits per month
- Has mailing list of 12,000+ people
- Has 4,000-name email mailing list of people interested in his work and who receive his monthly email newsletter
- Has toll-free number (800.381.2374)
- Licensed Mental Health Professional, Certified Professional Counselor, and Licensed Marriage and Family Therapist

Comments on Bill's books, public speaking, and marketing abilities

Sample book endorsements for previous trade books:
"*Love Is a Verb* is an excellent resource for anyone who wants to have a healthy relationship. It is a practical and simple guidebook to follow because its authors are experienced

teachers. They show you how to change and produce results."
> —Bernie Siegel, M.D., author of *Love, Medicine and Miracles* [Dr. Siegel requested five copies of the book in prepublication form for his five grown children]

"O'Hanlon's deceptively simple techniques can be used to produce remarkable and powerful change. *Do One Thing Different* is engaging and easy to read and equally valuable for clients and therapists alike. It's destined to be a classic."
> —Lonnie Barbach, Ph.D., author of *For Yourself, For Each Other* and *The Pause*

Comment from previous publicist:
"Bill O'Hanlon is a publicist's dream! I have thoroughly enjoyed working with him on his publicity for *Do One Thing Different*. He is professional, flexible, and readily available for anything that comes along. Bill is the type of author that makes a publicist's job worth it!"
> –Jennifer Heeseler, Publicist, Krupp Kommunications, January 2001

Comments from lecture attendees:
"Mr. O'Hanlon is the Seinfeld of psychotherapy, combining humor and solid technique to facilitate change."
> —Debbie Innocenti, MA, Ridgewood, NJ

"Without a doubt, the most infectiously enthusiastic presenter I've ever seen."
> —James Shelton, CAC, NCACII, Ridgewood, NJ

"It's simply the best, most instructive, and pragmatic presentation I've attended."
    —Stephen Woodstock, MA, Montclair, NJ

"Thank you—I do definitely feel validated for my beliefs of *optimism* in treatment. You are truly an expert public speaker. Your stories are *truly* enlightening."
    —Erin P. Solkowski-McGrath, LCSW, Darien, IL

"I feel this was one of the best workshops I've ever attended. Bill seems so at ease and the material just flows."
    —Yvonne Homan, LCSW, Evanston, IL

"Would love to get more and more. Personally available, responsive and giving—absence of the rampant malady which afflicts many presenters: The Voracious Ego Monster. Thorough; organized; entertaining."
    —Reid Whiteside, Ph.D., Raleigh, NC

"This was *the* best workshop I've ever attended. Very entertaining as well as informative and useful."
    —Shay Stanton, MSW, Hamilton, NJ

"One of the best workshops I ever attended in my 21 professional years."
    —Patrick Cacacie, ACSW, Trenton, NJ

TABLE OF CONTENTS
"You will not grow if you sit in a beautiful flower garden, but

you will grow if you are sick, if you are in pain, if you experience losses."
—Elizabeth Kubler-Ross

Introduction: Problems Are Opportunities in Drag: The Necessity and Value of Crises and Breakdowns

Chapter 1: Where Are We Going and Why Am I in This Handbasket? Crises, Breakdowns, Addictions, and Impasses as Signals and Callings to a Different Life

Chapter 2: Acknowledging: Or the Truth Shall Set You Free, but First It Will Piss You Off or Scare the Hell Out of You

Chapter 3: The Shadow Knows: Embracing and Allowing the Stuff You Are Ashamed and Afraid Of

Chapter 4: Follow Your Wound: Finding an Opening to the Future from What Has Injured or Hurt You in the Past

Chapter 5: Double Your Weirdness: Celebrating Your Uniqueness and Becoming a Proud Deviant

Chapter 6: Pissed or Blissed: How to Figure Out What You Are Supposed to Do With Your Life

Chapter 7: To Be and Not to Be, That Is the Invitation: The Power and Energy of Including Your Contradictions and Complexity

Chapter 8: Indiana Jones Meets Kierkegaard: Faith vs. Positive Thinking

Chapter 9: Walking Through the Room of 1,000 Demons: Taking Action in the Face of Your Fears and Limiting Beliefs

Chapter 10: The World as Your Guru: Letting Reality and Other People Teach You What Works (and What Doesn't)

Chapter 11: It's Hard to See the Spot You're Standing On: Recognizing and Challenging Premises and Automatic Patterns

Chapter 12: Having a Nervous Breakthrough: Key Points in Finding the Positive Benefits of Crises (Including How to Avoid Unnecessary Breakdowns)

Chapter Summaries

The Only Way Out Is Through

Introduction: Problems Are Opportunities in Drag: The Necessity and Value of Crises and Breakdowns

"Sometimes we climb the ladder all the way to the top, only to discover that we have placed it against the wrong wall."
—Joseph Campbell

Summary: This first section introduces the notion that breakdowns can be valuable. Most of us try to avoid crises and problems, but sometimes, when it is time to make a big life change or mid-course correction, a breakdown—a crisis big enough to overwhelm our usual coping mechanisms and defenses—may be necessary to help us make the change we know is needed.

Topics covered:

- The necessity of breakdowns
- Why usual solutions and coping or avoidance mechanisms won't work in some situations

- The promise of the book: to show the reader how to understand the importance and value of breakdowns and how to use breakdowns as breakthroughs

Chapter 1: Where Are We Going and Why Am I in This Handbasket? Crises, Breakdowns, Addictions, and Impasses as Signals and Callings to a Different Life

"If your train is on the wrong track, every station you come to is the wrong station."
—Bernard Malamud

Summary: Your current life and success strategies can take you only so far before they no longer work. Both the productive strategies and unhealthy patterns that got you to the place you are now are often insufficient to carry you into the future. Perhaps you have always avoided conflict, or you have developed the pattern of taking care of everyone else, or you have become rational and cut off your emotions. There are pros and cons to such strategies and patterns. They work in some contexts for some time, but in the end, they often break down. That aggressive sales style may work fine at work, but it is a disaster in your marriage. When their strategies stop working, people often keep themselves distracted by staying busy or they numb themselves with drugs, alcohol, or food. Drug and alcohol use, overworking, or overeating only work up to a point and then those also come crashing down. Health problems ensue, someone close to you dies or leaves the relationship, you get fired, you find out you owe thousands of more dollars in taxes than you expected and will have to work even harder to pay it off. We have developed patterns and beliefs that are limiting our lives by keeping us too restricted. The next phases in our lives will require more resources than we currently have available, but in order to change, most of us need to confront a crisis so large that we can't merely accommodate anymore; we must change. Internal and external crises can crack us open in painful but good ways, helping us rediscover what we have left behind and what we need for the next parts of our life journey.

Rainer Maria Rilke wrote evocatively of this kind of breakdown: *It's possible I am pushing through solid rock . . . I am such a long way in I see no way through, and no space: everything is close to my face, and everything close to my face is stone. I don't have much knowledge yet in grief—so this massive darkness makes me small. You be the master: make yourself fierce, break in: then your great transforming will happen to me, and my great grief cry will happen to you.*

Topics covered:

- Success strategies and coping mechanisms as attempted solutions that don't work forever
- Breakdowns and breakthroughs
- Wakeup calls
- Problems as signals and callings from the soul
- Straws that break your back and break you open
- When you can no longer go on like you have
- Addictions, numbing, and reawakening
- Crises as invitations to questioning your current life and future

Chapter 2: Acknowledging: Or the Truth Shall Set You Free, but First It Will Piss You Off or Scare the Hell Out of You

"We don't need to learn how to let things go, we just need to learn to recognize when they've already gone."
—Suzuki Roshi

Summary: This chapter will show that if we have turned away from ourselves, everything we do has some weird failure in it, even if we are outwardly successful. Sometimes the lives we are living are too small for our souls. We have accommodated in little ways through the years and the accumulation of those small accommodations has come at a large price over time. A senior executive, during a meeting on change in the workplace, was inspired to write a short poem. She stood up and read the poem: *Ten years ago, I turned my face for a moment . . . and it became my life.* The room went silent, as many of the other executives there contemplated the fact that they too found themselves in outwardly successful lives that they hated and wondered how their lives had gotten to such a place. We pay a cost when we live lives that we are not meant to live in exchange for security, money, acceptance, and so forth. If you go too far afield from a life that has meaning and passion for you, you will be stalked by your soul, which is calling you back to the life you were meant to lead and which will create or seize upon crises to invite you to re-examine and change your life.

The first step on the road back to the life you are meant to lead or to facing difficult issues, then, is to acknowledge where you are, which at first will probably frighten or upset you. In this chapter, you will learn that if you have gone off course, the truth you will face may be uncomfortable for you and others because it will require saying and doing things that you have been avoiding and that may be scary or painful and unfamiliar. It may be hard and disruptive initially, but it can also be exhilarating and enlivening. Telling the truth, to yourself or others, is the first step out of the life that no longer works. Most people will not tell the truth until a crisis (heart attack, cancer, an affair, loss of a job, severe depression, etc.) forces the issue.

Topics covered:

- How we get off course in life
- Accommodations for love or security
- Alien voices of others that we incorporate as our own
- The price we pay for lives of safety and security
- Your soul will not give up on you and will tug at your sleeve or stomp on your toe to get your attention
- Your soul can use crises to get you to finally tell the truth and make major changes when you haven't

Chapter 3: The Shadow Knows: Embracing and Allowing the Stuff You Are Ashamed and Afraid Of

"There seems to be some connection between the places we have disowned inside ourselves and the key to where we need to go. Life as usual has arranged a way in which we're not allowed to leave anything behind that is not somehow resolved."
—David Whyte, *"Poetry and the Imagination"*

Summary: This chapter tells you how you have become less than a 360-degree self, diminishing or leaving parts of yourself behind or hiding them from others. You sliced off a wedge here, accommodated to fit in, another wedge there to have security, another one to be loved, another one because you decided some part of you was unacceptable, and so on. What you end up with is a 270-degree self. Or a 180-degree self. So much of you goes missing that when it comes time to make a change or transition to a new phase of your life, you may not have the resources to make the transition. What you don't make room for in yourself has a life of its own and, if unacknowledged, will run you from underground, showing up as a compulsion (see Jimmy Swaggart or Bill Clinton as examples of people who have left their healthy sexuality behind, only to find sexuality creeping up on them and getting them in trouble). In order to reclaim the missing bits, you need to be able to acknowledge, be aware of, and explore the shadow sides of yourself.

Robert Bly reminds us in the following poem that we sometimes have to go through some dark and difficult places if we want to live.

Warning to the Reader (Robert Bly)
[poem omitted here due to copyright restrictions]

Topics covered:

- The costs of shaving off unacceptable aspects of self
- Through the rat's hole to wholeness

Chapter 4: Follow Your Wound: Finding an Opening to the Future from What Has Injured or Hurt You in the Past

"There is a crack in everything. That's how the light gets in."
    —Leonard Cohen

Summary: This chapter will show how the very things that have wounded us can be openings into the life we are moving toward. "Follow your bliss," Joseph Campbell said. *Bliss* derives from the French *blessure*, which means wound or injury. "Follow your wound," I say. Your emotional wounds, analogous to physical ones, are the openings from your skin (your closed-in self-protected world). What wounds us often drives us and gives us the focus to succeed or to overcome past pains. Robin Williams, the comedian, spent countless lonely hours as a child, making up characters and scenes to amuse himself. Later, this became the basis of his manic and amazing talent. Our wounds can also be the source of compassionate connection to others, as when Candy Lightener, a mother whose child was killed by a drunk driver, founded Mothers Against Drunk Driving (MADD) to try to prevent others from having to experience the devastating loss she did.

Topics covered:

- How our wounds and past hurts can be the very things that lead to a life of greatest aliveness
- Our skills and healthy obsessions often derive from our pain and problems

Chapter 5: Double Your Weirdness: Celebrating Your Uniqueness and Becoming a Proud Deviant

*"The physicist Leo Szilard once announced to his friend Hans Bethe that he was thinking of keeping a diary: 'I don't intend to publish it; I am merely going to record the facts for the information of God.' 'Don't you think God knows the facts?' Bethe asked. 'Yes,' said Szilard. 'He knows the facts, but he does not know **this version of the facts**.'"*
—Gilbert and Mulkay, *"Opening Pandora's Box"*

Summary: Each person is entirely unique. One of the expressions of that uniqueness is to find your voice, your own viewpoint, your idiosyncratic version of the facts, your singular way of articulation. This is the outward expression of your soul, of your wound, of yourself. I heard a story about Neil Young, the singer/songwriter. With many other Canadian singers, he was participating in a benefit recording, the Canadian version of "We Are the World," for hunger relief. Each of them had his or her own line to sing. During the playback, the producer stopped the tape after Neil Young's line and said rather sheepishly, "Neil, you were slightly off-pitch during your line. Let's do it over." To which Young replied: "Hey, man, that's my *style*!" When I heard that story, I thought, *Now that's a man who has found his voice and embraced his deviance.* No one else sings like he does and he's not ashamed of it, even if it is slightly off-pitch. Martha Graham, the innovative dancer, put it this way: *There is a vitality, a life force, an energy, a quickening that is translated though you into action—and because there is only one of you in all of time, this expression is unique. And*

*if you block it, it will never exist through any other medium
and be lost. The world will not have it. It is not your business
to determine how good it is nor how it compares with other
expressions. It is your business to keep it yours, clearly and
directly.* Finding your unique voice or style and becoming a
happy, shameless, and proud deviant (and I mean that in the
best sense of the word) can be another step back on the road to
the life you were meant to live.

Topics covered:

- Finding your voice and uniqueness
- Using your voice

Chapter 6: Pissed or Blissed: How to Figure Out What You Are Supposed to Do With Your Life

*"This is the true joy in life, the being used up for a purpose
recognized by yourself as a mighty one; the being a force of
nature instead of a feverish, selfish little clod of ailments and
grievances, complaining that the world will not devote itself to
making you happy. I am of the opinion that my life belongs to the
community, and as long as I live, it is my privilege to do for it
whatever I can. I want to be thoroughly used up when I die, for
the harder I work the more I live. I rejoice in life for its own sake.
Life is no 'brief candle' to me. It is a sort of splendid torch which
I have got hold of for a moment, and I want to make it burn as
brightly as possible before handing it on to future generations."*

—George Bernard Shaw, *"Man and Superman,"*
Act III, *"Don Juan in Hell"*

Summary: This chapter brings together the two previous chapters, connecting your wounds (what drives you) and your voice (your unique expression) into a mission or vision of what you can contribute to the world or other people. Each of us has unique contributions to make to the world, whether it be raising children, making a beautiful and peaceful garden in the back-yard, inventing new computer chips, singing wonderful songs, working to eliminate world hunger, preserving seeds of dying plant species, preventing drunk-driving deaths, publishing fine books—a big or small mission. These are things that make our hearts sing; not just what feels good, but a higher calling. Discovering your destiny can make life meaningful and help you bear the hurts and frustrations inherent in life. This chapter will give readers clues about how they can find their destinies and callings. The two major ways to discover what you are meant to do in this life is to pay attention to what blisses you out (what compels you, gives you energy, or brings your heart and soul alive) and/or what pisses you off (what injustice in the world or your life bothers you and you feel driven to correct or address). **[See sample writing attached to this proposal for this chapter.]**

Topics covered:

- Pissed or Blissed: Two sure-fire ways to identify your passion and destiny
- Discovering your destiny, purpose, meaning, and contribution

Chapter 7: To Be and Not to Be, That Is the Invitation: The Power and Energy of Including Your Contradictions and Complexity

"Do I contradict myself? Very well, then I contradict myself, I am large, I contain multitudes."
     —Walt Whitman

Summary: One of the ways to get back the missing wedges in the 360-degree self is to revalue previously devalued aspects of one's self. Another is to embrace and allow contradictions within one's experience. You may have a pattern of leaving relationships when the going gets tough or of being a "nice guy" when you need to be firm. The inclusive self is the place where you can feel like leaving but you stay. Or you can feel like you want to be a nice guy but still be tough. Instead of reacting as you usually do and staying with your usual patterns and habits, this chapter will show you a way to reclaim and embrace more of yourself, even contradictions within yourself, to come more fully alive. This also helps you challenge patterns that keep producing the same (unwanted) results in your life. You will then have more resources available to meet the next crisis you encounter, rather than having it stop you or break you down.

Topics covered:

- Reconnecting with the 360-degree self
- Reclaiming the missing pieces

- Embracing and including seeming contradictions or opposites
- Permission, validation, and inclusion
- The inclusive self

Chapter 8: Indiana Jones Meets Kierkegaard: Faith vs. Positive Thinking

"Faith is the ability to look at the world we have created and see possibility, even as we acknowledge our capacity for destruction. It is the glue that holds our fractured pieces together and allows us to continue beyond all reason. The faith we seek is not the comfort of having all the answers. Rather, it is the will to keep asking the questions. Faith is the voice in the night that says we will go on."

—Catherine Whitney

Summary: This chapter is an examination of the difference between positive thinking ("Every day in every way, things are getting better") and what I call the Possibility Stance ("Some days in some ways, things are getting better and in some ways, things are getting worse"). Then, armed with this more inclusive and realistic stance, you step out into the unknown with the possibility that things can work out—because not to step out would be to remain paralyzed and to step out with a "positive attitude" might lead to stepping foolishly and blindly off the cliff (like the Fool on the Hill or Pollyanna).

Topics covered:

- The Possibility Stance—Not positive or negative thinking
- Acknowledging reality and stepping into possibility: Indiana Jones and the leap of faith
- Acting even when things look impossible or bad
- The difference between Indiana Jones and Kierkegaard: Creating the future through acts of faith

Chapter 9: Walking Through the Room of 1,000 Demons: Taking Action in the Face of Your Fears and Limiting Beliefs

"I was afraid of lightning storms when I was a little girl. If one came up in the night, I'd go get into bed with my mama. I'd wait for a flash of lightning to show me the way to her room. I still remember the strange feeling of standing there in the dark waiting for the thing I was afraid of. Sometimes it's the things that scare us the most that get us to a place where we're safer. But knowing that doesn't make the trip any easier."
    —Lilly, in *"I'll Fly Away"*

*"You gain strength, courage and confidence by every experience in which you really stop to look fear in the face. . . . You **must** do the thing you think you cannot do."*
    —Eleanor Roosevelt

Summary: You can acknowledge fear and not let it stop you. Fear is a great advisor and a poor master. When you feel afraid of physical danger, it is important to attend to and act on that fear. But too many people let unnecessary fears that have nothing to do with physical safety stop them from moving in the direction of aliveness and authenticity. The poet David Whyte tells about a time when he was traveling in the Himalayas with some companions. David decided to take a particularly arduous course over a mountain path and his companions decided they would take a route that would take two days longer to reach their mutual destination. Well into his hike, David came across a cable bridge over a deep ravine. One side of the cable had snapped and the bridge's slats had accordioned together. Up to that time, David had been a fairly fearless hiker and climber, but the bridge looked too scary to him, and something in him stopped him from going on. He sat and talked to himself, telling himself that it was foolish to be so afraid, that he should just go across. After about an hour, however, he finally realized he wasn't going to be able to get himself to go across the bridge. He would have to go back the way he came, losing a day and causing his friends to worry about his safety when he wasn't on time to meet them. But as he turned around, he came face to face with a wizened little old Tibetan woman who was coming up the path with a basket of yak dung she had been collecting tucked under her arm. She greeted him with a bow and quickly limped past him over the bridge. Without a thought, he turned to follow her. Many of us come to a similar bridge in our own lives. We cannot get ourselves to go on. We stop. This chapter offers some hints for recognizing and dealing with those fears and limiting beliefs we have about ourselves and life and crossing the chasm we are terrified to cross.

Topics covered:

- How to recognize unhelpful fears and limiting beliefs
- How to stop fear or unhelpful beliefs from determining or dominating your life

Chapter 10: The World as Your Guru: Letting Reality and Other People Teach You What Works (and What Doesn't)

"Cloquette hated reality. But she realized it was still the only place you could get a good steak."
—Woody Allen

"Ever tried? Ever failed? No matter. Try again. Fail again. Fail better."
—Samuel Beckett

Summary: If you pay attention, the world and other people can show and teach you all you need to know to follow your destiny and live the life you were meant to live. Observe the responses of the world; adjust your actions accordingly and find mentors or models for the things you haven't a clue about.

Beatrix Potter, the creator of Peter Rabbit and other children's stories, wanted to be a nature illustrator but was blocked in this goal by the sexism of British society, which held that a woman could not be an illustrator. Publishers refused even to look at her illustrations, although they were some of the best of the day. She was distraught until the woman who was previously her nanny, who had left to get married and have children, informed Ms. Potter that she never threw out the illustrated letters with pictures of animals and stories Ms. Potter had sent her children over the years. The children had asked to see and hear them again and again. Ms. Potter asked for the letters back and put her first children's book together from the material in them, leading to a successful and satisfying career in which she could use her illustration skills.

Most of what you do is bound to fail, but that's okay, because the only way to discover what works is to make mistakes, fail a lot, and learn. The only way to fail a lot is to move into action, because the world only responds to what you do. Michael Jordan, the basketball star who one year was cut from his high school basketball team because he wasn't good enough, came back the next year having practiced diligently all summer and overcome some of his weaknesses. He says this: *I have missed more than 9,000 shots in my career. I have lost almost 300 games. On 26 occasions I have been entrusted to take the game winning shot . . . and I missed. I have failed over and over and over again in my life. And that is precisely . . . why I succeed.*

Topics covered:

- The world as your teacher and guru
- Models and mentors as guides
- Discover what the world wants and needs
- Take massive action toward the desired outcome
- Make mistakes
- Notice the results of your actions
- Make adjustments in action

Chapter 11: It's Hard to See the Spot You're Standing On: Recognizing and Challenging Premises and Automatic Patterns

"When you discover you are riding a dead horse, the best strategy is to dismount."
　　　　—Dakota tribal saying

Summary: Sometimes we think thoughts, sometimes they think us. This chapter will alert you to the automatic interpretations, patterns, and beliefs you walk around with and how to step aside and examine, rather than be dominated by these ideas, habits, and beliefs. The reader will discover ways to get off automatic pilot and start to choose ways to act and be rather than to be determined by the past or beliefs.

Topics covered:

- Recognizing and challenging unexamined and unhelpful beliefs, interpretations, and patterns
- Recognizing thoughts that think you and starting to think for yourself
- Acting freely rather than from old, unproductive habits and patterns

One Source of Bad Information (Robert Bly)
[poem omitted due to copyright restrictions]

Chapter 12: Having a Nervous Breakthrough: Key Points in Finding the Positive Benefits of Crises (Including How to Avoid Unnecessary Breakdowns)

"Security is mostly superstition. It does not exist in nature nor do the children of men as a whole experience it. Avoiding danger is no safer in the long run than outright exposure. Life is either a daring adventure or it is nothing."
—Helen Keller

Summary: This chapter is a send-off with a summary of the journey the reader has just taken. We get off course when we go on automatic pilot, living lives that are too much determined by our fears, old programming, and patterns we have fallen into to be accepted and gain security. This can lead to unhappiness and crises that break us down. But a life of aliveness and passion is always available to us and we have all the tools we need to get back to such a life. Our souls will help us, waiting patiently for a crisis or deliberately creating a crisis, to call our current life into question and lead us back to a life of integrity and authenticity. We can discover how to make success from the very mistakes and wounds we have. Then we can reclaim our voices, our destinies, and passion and make the kind of contribution to the world that we are here to make. We can even learn to avoid major crises and breakdowns if we listen to ourselves and our soul and let it keep us on the path that we are meant to walk. Antonio Machado, the Spanish poet, says it well in this poem.

Last night, as I was sleeping (Antonio Machado)
[poem omitted due to copyright restrictions]

Topics covered:

- Trust your soul
- Tell the truth about where you are and who you are
- Face your fears and do not let them determine what you do
- Connect with the things and people that bring you alive or engage your passion (even what pisses you off or upsets you)
- Develop a compassionate relationship with yourself, accepting and including your flaws and contradictions
- When you know your destiny and calling, take massive action to make your dreams real in the world
- Be willing to be uncomfortable, not to know, and to make mistakes
- Step outside your usual patterns and beliefs
- Observe the results of your actions and be flexible enough to change them when they are not working
- You can avoid breakdowns and major crises if you listen to yourself deeply and follow your soul

I left the sample writing section from this proposal out of this book for space purposes, but it was included in the original proposal. Beginning authors should include two or three chapters of sample writing from the book. They should be representative. If there are cartoons or illustrations in some of the chapters, make sure you include some in the sample chapters. If you will include exercises, include at least one exercise example in your sample writing.

You don't necessarily have to include the first two or three chapters. The sample chapters may be from the middle or end of the book as well. Choose strong and representative material.

PROPOSAL CHECKLIST

Use this list to ensure you have included all the elements needed to deliver a complete proposal for your nonfiction book.

A few general notes: Your proposal should be very business-like. No fancy fonts (Times New Roman is safe). No colored paper (unless your project is a graphic book that would need color to illustrate how it will look). Use plain white paper with no smudges. Also, allow no typos. Go over it again and again and get others to look it over to eliminate any typos or grammatical errors. And, everything should be double-spaced.

✓ **Title page:** This is the easiest. Create one page with the words "Book Proposal" at the top. Put the title in the middle of the page followed by the subtitle. Then add a line space to indicate a new section and put your name and contact information (address, email, telephone number) on it. If you have an agent, then put his or her contact information on it instead.

✓ **Introduction:** This is a brief overview of the book and of you. What genre is this book? Why is it needed; what hole in the marketplace does it fill? Why is there an audience for the book and who are they? Who are you and why are you the best person to write this book and publicize it? What credibility and accomplishments do you have relevant to this book? Try to keep this to one or two pages, or as concise as possible to get the point across effectively.

✓ **Chapter outline/chapter summaries:** This can be two sections or one. You could just list the chapters in a short section to give the reader an overview or you could fold that in to your chapter summaries. I prefer the latter. Give the chapter title (and subtitle, if you have one) for each chapter, followed by a short (two- or three-sentence) description of what the chapter will be about. Then provide two to four bullet points summarizing highlights of the chapter.

✓ **Manuscript specifications:** This is a short paragraph in which you specify how many pages (or words) your book will be, whether it will need any special formatting or permissions (for illustrations, cartoons, excerpts from other copyrighted works, and so on) and what your time-line for delivering the manuscript will be.

✓ **The competition:** Here you should list three to five other books that are similar to yours and that have succeeded in the marketplace. Give their titles, the authors' names, their publication dates, and the publishers' names. Then compare and contrast each to your book, showing why you are filling an unmet need in the marketplace. Don't put the other books down too much; just explain why your book is different and fills a hole that no other book has filled.

✓ **Platform statement/marketing plan:** Here you should list all your accomplishments relating to the book, why you are qualified to write it, and any abilities you have to get the word out about the book once it is published. If you have any pre-endorsements from well-known people, include them here as well. Provide your thought-out marketing plan in this section.

✓ **Sample writing:** Include two or three chapters to give an idea of your writing style and ability, as well as what a typical chapter will look like (for example, if you will use cartoons or illustrations, your sample writing should include those).

✓ **Supplemental materials:** Include in your proposal package any supporting evidence for your marketing abilities and accomplishments. This could include short audio or video excerpts from media appearances (any will do, but the more relevant to the book's content, the better), proof of any fan following you have (email newsletter subscriber numbers, Twitter followers, Facebook fan numbers, and so on).

That's it. Now get cracking and get that proposal put together so your book can get out into the world.

Proposal Completion Commitments

I intend to complete my title page by _____

Title page completed

I intend to complete my overview and introduction by _____

Overview and introduction completed

I intend to complete my author bio by _____

Author bio completed

I intend to complete my manuscript specifications section by _____

Manuscript specifications section completed

I intend to complete my chapter outline by _____

Chapter outline completed

I intend to complete my chapter summaries by _____

Chapter summaries completed

I intend to complete my platform statement by _____

Platform statement completed

I intend to complete my market analysis and competitive titles section by _____

Market analysis and competitive titles section completed

I intend to complete my sample writing by _____

Sample writing completed

FINAL WORDS ABOUT PROPOSALS

Mastering the art of proposal writing is a separate skill from writing books. It requires that you step back and take a birds-eye view of the book project and also that you take the long view, seeing the book from conception through publication. It requires that you think not just as a creative person/writer but as a hard-headed marketer who looks with dispassionate eyes on your book as a product.

That's why, even if you are self-publishing, preparing a proposal will probably help you. And, of course, if you intend to sell your book to a publisher, having that proposal is crucial.

If you are seeking a publisher or an agent, you should send a "query letter," a short letter introducing yourself and your book project, and wait for a positive response before sending your proposal. Fiction and memoir writers should send a query letter and wait for a positive response before sending their more extensive writing samples as well. Some agents and publishers accept email queries, but do some research first to see if someone would be open to this.

Also, please note that some publishers have specific proposal formats posted on their websites. In that case, adapt what I have given you here to use their format.

Finally, here are some books that are solid if you really want to go more deeply into learning about proposals.

Books on Proposals

Eckstut, Arielle, and David Sterry. (2005). *Passion Into Print: Get Your Book Published Successfully.* New York, NY: Workman.

Herman, Jeff, and Deborah Levine Herman. (2001). *Write the Perfect Book Proposal: 10 That Sold and Why.* New York, NY: John Wiley and Sons.

Maisel, Eric. (2004). *The Art of the Book Proposal: From Focused Idea to Finished Proposal.* New York, NY: Tarcher/Penguin.

Page, Susan. (1997). *The Shortest Distance Between You and a Published Book.* New York, NY: Broadway.

CHAPTER 4

How a Busy Therapist Can Write a Book
Overcoming Busyness, Barriers, and Avoidance

As an author, I often have people approach me and offer a "great idea" for a book. They propose that I write it and we share credit and royalties. I laugh and tell them, "Ideas are easy to come by. It's the act of putting those ideas on paper that is the hard work." It's the actual process of planning, then writing your book, that is the difference between people who write books and those who merely have good ideas.

In this chapter, you will learn how to get your book written amid your busy life and practice. I'll help you get moving with your writing and overcome any barriers, fears, blocks, and procrastination when it comes to getting your writing done. I have read hundreds of books about writing now and they all have different advice as to how you can get your book written. What I take from that is that there is no one way that works for everyone.

Many writing books tell you that, to succeed as an author, you have to write every day. I've never written every day in my entire writing life and this is my 34th book, so I guess they are wrong about that.

In this chapter, I will offer you a smorgasbord of possibilities that might help you get your book written and completed.

Pick and choose among the options. If you find one thing in this chapter that helps you move forward or get your book completed, it will have been worth my while to write it and yours to read it.

BARRIERS TO WRITING

Having taught and coached many people to write books over the years, I have heard all the reasons, barriers, and fears about writing that there are.

Here's a pretty good list. I will wait for a moment while you find yours among the list.

- I'm too busy.
- I'll never get published so why bother?
- I don't know where to start.
- I'm afraid of rejection.
- I'm afraid of being exposed.
- I'm not a good writer.
- I have to know everything about my subject before I write a book.
- It has to be perfect.
- I have nothing original to say.
- I will get sued or lose my license when I write about other people.

Okay, now we're going to basically ignore whatever reason (or reasons) jumped out at you while you read this chapter.

I think writing is done by unreasonable people. By that, I mean that people who write and publish books have those same reasons why they couldn't, can't, shouldn't, or won't write. They just found a way to write in spite of the reasons.

So, let me tell you what I know about how to get books written rather than spend a lot of time trying to get you past your fears and barriers by discussing them directly.

HOW TO WRITE YOUR BOOK
Be Willing to Suck

Isabel Allende was a successful novelist when she was asked to lead a writing class. She soon discovered that although she knew how to get good writing from herself, she clearly didn't know how to evoke it from others. The students' writing was stilted and pedantic. She finally realized they were all trying too hard and getting in their own ways. So, she announced that the goal for the class was to write not the "Great American Novel" but the "Worst American Novel." They should strive for mediocrity. With this instruction, several students relaxed and ended up writing something publishable.

I mentioned earlier that having a contract and knowing that the book will be published is a great motivator for me. I have only written one book without a contract. I woke up one night and had a great idea for a book. I got up and wrote out a rough outline. I happened to have some time off (I try to take a month off every August), so I began to write the book. To my amazement, my fingers began flying over the keyboards so fast I could barely keep up. The writing was funny, irreverent, and lively. My books before that had a little humor in them, but their main trait was that the ideas were very clear and useful for readers. I am pretty funny and irreverent in my everyday life, but I am a bit more "straight" and serious in my books. With this book, I had finally found my style. It was a bit different than my speaking voice but was closer than I had gotten in previous writing. I finished the first draft in a week (it was a short book, which ultimately doomed it to being an e-book, as my agent and publishers decided it was not long enough and I loved it just the length it was).

I think what freed me up was that I wasn't worried about whether it would be published or what my agent or publisher might think of it. Whether that book ever got published was not as relevant as the floodgates of thought it opened. Writing has been easier for me ever since.

Whatever you think you "should" do when you write or how you "should" write could be the thing that is holding you back from freely writing or writing as well as you could.

So give yourself permission to suck at writing. I mentioned before that with most of my early books, most of the writing was really rewriting. Get the book written. Fix it in the mix. Get the words down without having that inner critic looking over your shoulder by telling him or her that what you are writing doesn't have to be good; it only has to get done. You can edit it later or decide you won't publish it.

Here is an experiment you can try. Write something that you promise yourself no one will ever see or read. You might even have to make a plan to burn it right after you finish it to reassure yourself enough to break free. Write it just as you want, without regard to other people's opinions or the rules you have learned. Break any and all of those rules. Write with bad grammar or run-on sentences. Write in all capital letters. Swear up a storm. Be politically incorrect. Tell your deepest, most shameful secrets or fantasies. Spill the beans on your family or your patients. Be mean. Whine and be self-indulgent. Break all the rules that your critical mind and conscience give you.

The Solution-Oriented Method: Use What Has Worked to Get Your Writing Done

I created an approach to therapy called "solution-oriented therapy," in which the therapist and client investigate what works in a client's life and then apply that to the problem to solve it. This is sort of the mirror image of the Woody Allen approach, which involves analyzing your problems and the source of them for decades, hoping for good mental health to result. There is research that indicates people are more creative when they focus on pleasant experiences rather than on painful or upsetting ones. Let's apply this idea to writing and completing your book.

One simple way to discover what works is to think back on the times you have done anything well or succeeded at something. I call this finding your contexts of competence. In what settings are things relatively easy for you? In what contexts do you feel a sense of mastery or at least competence? In what areas have you accomplished something that was difficult?

I was working with one writer who was daunted by the task, when I found out he was a dedicated golfer. I asked him what he had learned on the golf course that he could apply in his writing. He thought for a minute and answered that he always did best when he cleared his mind of everything but the golf game. He didn't think about all the undone errands or problems at home or work. He just focused on being in the moment and hitting the ball. When I asked how he could apply that same skill to writing, he decided that he would slot out some time each week, as he did with golf, and borrow a friend's office (it would be vacant at the same time each week, he knew, because his friend played golf several days a week at the same time) to get some quiet uninterrupted time where he could focus his attention only on writing.

Another would-be writer had survived breast cancer. She had gotten through it by focusing on herself and her needs, instead of following her usual pattern of taking care of everyone else. As we discussed how she could use this hard-won knowledge to get her book written, she realized she was going to have to tell several friends that she was not going to be available for the long talks they were used to having with her about their current problems. Doing so would free up several hours each week that she could use for writing.

Are you getting the pattern of this solution-oriented approach toward writing? Think of an area in which you feel confident or in which you succeeded. Then consider how you developed that confidence. Or think of how you operate in that environment. Or remember how you overcame the odds to achieve something. Then consider how you might use or adapt those success strategies to your writing.

✎ The Solution-Oriented Method of Writing Worksheet ✎

1. Write down some area in which you have succeeded, accomplished something, feel confident, or are competent.

2. Write down how you succeeded or got confident in that area. What methods, skills, attitudes, or strategies do you or did you use in that area?

3. Was there a time you can remember in which writing came relatively easily or quickly?

4. Was there a time when your writing was particularly good?

5. Was there a time when you were chomping at the bit to get started writing rather than procrastinating or avoiding?

6. How might you transfer the skills, attitudes, knowledge, confidence, competence, or strategies from that successful area to any place in your writing life you might need them?

Another solution-oriented inquiry I use with writers is this: Where in life have you or do you transcend your feelings and get yourself to do difficult things? Sometimes writers don't feel like writing. Use what you know in other areas of your life to find the resources and strategies to transcend that reluctance and write anyway. Those of you who are parents probably know the scenario of being utterly exhausted and then having to wake up during the night to take care of a sick child. That definitely involves transcending your feelings of the moment to do what is best.

You've probably also done this sometime in your work life. Have you ever done a task at work you weren't into or didn't feel you had the energy or motivation to do? You did it because you wanted to keep getting paid or you were too timid to say no. Or perhaps you've said no to that piece of dessert you really wanted or turned down some alcohol or drugs when you knew they wouldn't serve you well in the long run.

My point is that you have developed the muscles of transcending your feelings of the moment to do something challenging. Use those muscles to do your writing when you don't feel like it or when you feel like doing something else that would be easier or more fun in the moment.

- Think about any and all moments when you haven't "gone with your feelings" in the moment but instead did something you knew you needed to accomplish or do.
- Use those same strategies the next time you don't feel like writing or are not inspired.

PATTERNS OF COMPLETING PROJECTS

Sometimes the issue is not writing but completing your book or writing project. You can also use the solution-oriented method to help with that.

When you have completed something, how did you do it? Did you work on it straight through without stopping? Did you recruit friends to help you? Did you do it one little step at a time? Did you draw out a map of the project before starting? Did you gather all the supplies you needed before starting? Did you do some of it, let it rest for a time, then go back to it? Did you do it in the early morning hours, late at night, or during the weekend?

One person I coached in one of my writing groups had built a backyard deck. It took him a while to finish it, but finish it he did. When he expressed concern that he wouldn't be able to complete a book, I asked him how he had finished the deck. He told me that he had bought a book about building decks and read that first, so he had the "big picture." Then he went and talked to someone at the local building supply store and got some specific pointers. Next, he made a list of the supplies he needed and bought them all, so that when he had time, he would be able to begin at once. On his first free weekend, he began. He worked steadily all weekend, breaking only for short meals. By the end of the first weekend, he had enough of it done so that it became self-reinforcing. He worked on it an hour or so each night after work and then finished it, with the help of a friend, the following weekend.

I suggested that he use the deck project as a template for getting his book done. He had already read a book or two about writing. He was attending one of my writing coaching groups when we had the discussion, so he had already done the first two steps. What supplies did he need to be ready to begin the project when he had time?

A new laptop computer and to set up a corner of his basement where he could write. He also needed an outline (he developed an outline during the course of the group, so that was another element achieved). He made a plan to start writing on his first unscheduled weekend, about a month from the time the group ended. He would enlist the help of a friend who was a good editor when he was about halfway done with his proposal and sample chapters. He would work every free weekend and one hour per night until his proposal was done.

Then he would use the same structure to complete the writing for his book. After going through this list, he said he knew he could write a book. It wasn't so daunting after all.

Here are the steps for this exercise:

1. Think of your patterns of finishing things and draw out the patterns from them. Write down every element or strategy you typically use. Use as many examples of finishing things you can. Combine the best of any or all of them.
2. Make a plan to use the same strategies and structures to get your writing project done.

Can you remember a time when you felt you had found your style, your voice, or your method, even though it was "all wrong"? What were the unique elements or methods you used at that time? Can you recreate or enhance that in your writing life?

Baby Steps, Baby Steps:
The Take the Small Steps Method

As Steven Wright famously said once, "I'm writing a book. I've got the page numbers down." One thing accomplished! Many therapists related to the movie *What About Bob?* and laughed at the pop psychiatrist's prescriptive program, Baby Steps. Take small steps out of problems and small steps into mental health. As silly as it sounded, many writers have successfully used the same strategy to get their writing done. A Chinese proverb also makes the point: Enough shovels of earth—a mountain. Enough pails of water—a river.

The title of Anne Lamott's popular writing book *Bird by Bird* derives from an anecdote she tells about when her brother was panicked after putting off doing a report on birds that was due the next day. When their father suggested the boy get going on the project, he cried, "But how will I ever do it?" "Bird by bird, buddy, bird by bird," was the father's calm reply.

Writing a book can seem so overwhelming to beginners that they sometimes avoid engaging in it. If you are in that category, try using the baby steps method. The first way to use it is to focus not on the whole task but on the smallest piece of the task you can. Even John Steinbeck used this strategy. Here's what he said: "When I face the desolate impossibility of writing 500 pages, a sick sense of failure falls on me, and I know I can never do it. Then gradually, I write one page and then another. One day's work is all I can permit myself to contemplate."

How can you divide your project up into bite-sized chunks?

Here's a possibility: After you make an outline, make a more detailed outline, with ideas for anecdotes, quotations, exercises, scenes, plot points, which characters are in the scene, where it takes place, and so on. Try to make it as detailed as possible. Then transfer each of those detailed points onto index cards that you can carry with you everywhere and then keep writing on. Keep the cards bundled with a rubber band in chapter or section order.

E. L. Doctorow describes his process of writing a book in such small steps terms: "It's like driving at night in the fog. You can only see as far as your headlights, but you can make the whole trip that way."

DIVIDING THE WRITING PROCESS INTO SMALL INCREMENTS OF TIME

A simple strategy for getting yourself to write when you are not writing is to commit to small amounts of time. A favorite choice for many writers is 5 minutes. This does not mean that you will write for only 5 minutes. It means you promise to write for at least 5 minutes per day or per writing session. You can write more if you want. But you must write at least 5 minutes. If you can get yourself to write a little, that trickle often turns into a flow. What is a realistic minimal amount of time you are willing to commit to writing each day or each week?

Because the human mind often works better with a limited and achievable finish line, I recommend that you make limited time commitments as well. You decide you'll write every day for one month or that you will write three times per week for two weeks. If it works for you and is producing the writing you want, you can recommit or commit to a longer time period. How long could you commit to that seems doable and not so daunting?

Most writers believe that it is important to write every day for the same reason. It shows them and the world that they take the job of writing seriously. It also seems to train the unconscious mind to be ready to write, and writers often report that they solve problems or come up with ideas in their dreams when they keep to such schedules.

If you are not inspired and the writing isn't coming, you might engage in some related tasks like backing up your writing on the computer, sharpening your pencils, or completing other little tasks that at least are in the realm of writing.

You can also commit to writing until you reach a certain goal, like two chapters, or 10,000 words. Then, after that, you can recommit to new quotas.

- What is a realistic small amount of writing (number of words or number of pages) you are willing to commit to writing each day or week?
- How long could you commit to so that it seems doable and not so daunting?

Blog Your Way to a Book

Blogs are one of the easiest ways to get your work out into the world and make yourself visible.

I was leading a speakers' boot camp some years ago and talking about how all wannabe speakers should have a website and a blog. I didn't actually have a blog at the time (and my speaking schedule was booked for years in advance, so I didn't have a lot of motivation to get one). Many of the participants groaned at my suggestion of creating a blog, because it sounded too technical. But another of the participants spoke up and said that setting up a blog was dead simple and that it could be done in less than 5 minutes. I told him not to exaggerate, that I was sure it was relatively easy but 5 minutes seemed unrealistic. He held his ground and offered to show everyone in the group how to set one up in less than 5 minutes. I and several other participants had our laptops with us and indeed, we had blogs set up within 4 minutes. It was literally several fill-in boxes and clicks. Easy as pie (easier, actually—pie takes more time and is more complicated).

But in addition to the visibility a blog can give you and your book, it can also be a way to write your book (or major parts of it) in little bits that you later compile into a book. Blog entries (called posts) are typically short (a few paragraphs or pages) and are published several times per week or month or as frequently as the blogger has time to do them.

One of the most famous examples of using a blog to write a book came from Julie Powell. She began blogging while working at an office in New York City. To spice up her life, she decided to try to cook recipes from Julia Child's *Mastering the Art of French Cooking* every evening for a year and to write about how the dinners came out. At first, only friends and family followed her blog, but soon, word spread far and wide. Her blog and project were featured in the media and offers of a book contract followed. Her book, *Julie and Julia: 365 Days, 524 Recipes, 1 Tiny Apartment Kitchen* was published by Little, Brown, became a bestseller, and was later turned into a movie starring Meryl Streep.

The blog "Baghdad Burning" (written during the early part of the American occupation of Iraq pseudonymously by an Iraqi woman who feared for her safety if her identity was revealed) was later turned into a book and went on to win the Samuel Johnson Prize in Britain, which awards $53,000.

Jessica Cutler created a juicy insider's gossip blog about Washington, DC, called "The Washingtonienne," which she turned into a novel and which was published by Hyperion in 2005.

A student of mine, Ron Kaiser, has taken blog entries written over the course of a year or so, polished them up, and is going to self-publish a book based on them. In the midst of his busy life and therapy practice, this was, he said, a great way to get a book written in bite-sized pieces and chunks of time.

So a blog could be a nice way to get yourself to write, every day or once a week. Even if your entire blog wouldn't translate perfectly into a book, you can take pieces of it to begin or create a book project. You will also get writing practice, and because blogs are so informal and can be revised at any time, you will probably lose some of that performance pressure many writers feel. In addition, if you make a mistake (in grammar or fact), your readers will surely let you know, in effect becoming your early editors. They might even suggest new topics or slants on things or bring up questions you hadn't considered.

Tip: Creating a blog is really quite simple. You can go to Word-Press.org and get the WordPress application installed on your site for free in about 5 minutes with a few clicks. I've done it many times and I am not that much of a techie. Ask your web-hosting site and it will probably have some simple instructions or even a short video that will walk you through the process. Or if that is too intimidating for you, ask a techie friend or family member to install it and show you how it works. It is only a little more complicated than using a word processor.

Warning: Blogs can be incredibly self-indulgent time sucks as well, so be wary. Sometimes you can't tell at first whether the blog will be a help or hindrance to your book-writing project. But if after some months, you find you are doing nothing with the book and the blog itself isn't going to turn into a book, drop it or do less blogging for a while and get yourself back to writing and preparing the book.

The Promise Method:
Use Commitments to Get Your Writing Done

I finished many of my early books through a combination of factors, one of which was a passionate desire to communicate. Another crucial element was that a publisher paid me money and I promised to deliver the manuscript by a specified date.

If I had promised myself that I would complete a book by a certain date, I might have finished it or I might not have. Too many times I have promised myself I will exercise daily or three times a week and then broken my vow after some time when I get busy or "don't feel like it." However, I rarely break my promises to other people, especially when they have paid me money and I have signed a legal contract.

In this respect, nonfiction writers are in a better position than fiction writers. I only have to write a small section of my proposed book, along with a summary and some marketing plans and I can sell the book before I have written it. Fiction writers usually have to write more of the book, sometimes the whole thing, in order to pre-sell it.

Combined with my intense desire to get the book out, this contractual obligation and the expectation of the publisher were sufficient to get my early projects completed and out the door. I don't need the element of the contract as much anymore (I have written several books without a contract in recent years), but it does usually give me a clear timeline for delivering the manuscript.

Even if you don't have a contract, though, you can use this method to help you finish your writing. What follows are several ways to use promises to get your writing done.

PROMISE SOMEONE ELSE

Someone who attended one of my writing and publishing boot camps said that she was there because she had promised her mentor on his deathbed that she would finally write the book that she had been hoping to write for many years. Who could you recruit to take you at your word for writing or finishing your book project? I am not talking about someone who will pile on the guilt if you don't write; rather, it should be someone who believes in you and your book and will be ruthlessly loyal to you in helping you get going, keep going, and ultimately finish.

I have coached people for some years on getting their writing done and have found some things that work and some traps to avoid in making promises. First, because you are a writer, perhaps I don't need to convince you of the power of words in making promises. Be careful of your language here. Self-help gurus and therapists have pointed out that certain phrases can set you up to fail or weasel out of commitments. Like Yoda in the Star Wars movies exhorts Luke Skywalker, "There is no try, only do." Other phrases to watch for: I'd like; I want to; someday; when I get enough time. Fill in your own weasel phrase here: _____.

At the end of my writing and publishing coaching groups, I have participants tell the group out loud what they intend to do and what they promise to do to get their books written and published. Some produce slippery phrases that don't really indicate a true commitment. They say, "I hope to have three chapters written by the end of the year." Or "I want to develop a habit of writing every day." I gently coach them to make more definitive statements. A promise is something you say you'll do, not think about doing, not just want to do or hope to do. If you were getting married and said, "I hope to love, honor, and obey" or "I want to be faithful," it probably wouldn't go over well with your intended. Or if you said to a friend, "I hope to meet you for dinner Thursday," your friend would get the sense you are not committed to being there. I regularly meet people who tell me things like, "I want to write a book" or "I hope to write a book someday." These, to my therapist's ear, are almost always indications that their books are unlikely to materialize.

So, what does a promise sound like? It uses definitive words, like "will," rather than waffling words or phrases. For example, "I will have my proposal done by December 31, 2013," instead of "I plan to have my proposal done by December 31, 2013."

Another element of effective promises is specificity. Instead of "My book will be done sometime in the next year," a true commitment is something like "My book will be done by October 1, 2014." There are two things to be specific about: specific actions or specific results. A specific action promise might be "I commit to writing at least 15 minutes a day, 6 days a week, for the next month." A specific result promise could be "I agree to have two chapters completed by August 3rd of this year."

Sometimes one has to get more specific about phrases or words that are not clearly specific and whose meanings might be ambiguous. For example, in the last promise above, what does the phrase "two chapters completed" mean? Does that mean drafts or finished, polished chapters that you would feel proud to send to an agent or editor? You might get specific on the number of words in the chapters or clarify any other ambiguity in the words or phrases in your promise.

Another element of effective promises can be writing them down and speaking them aloud to others. I tend to forget my promises. I'm good at keeping them if I write them down, but if I don't, I might keep them or I might not. Speaking them aloud seems important for some people. Making public commitments evokes a sense of responsibility or shame that helps them keep the commitments. I grew up Catholic and felt guilty about so many things, I think I have burned out too many shame cells in my brain, so this public shame stuff doesn't move me as much as it could.

I do well with another person helping to keep me on track, though. I call this person my accountability partner. He or she agrees to hear my promises and work out some procedures, usually regular check-ins by phone, in person, or by email, both to help remind me of my promise and to coach me through the hard parts of the project. My accountability partners don't use guilt but only provide encouraging reminders and brainstorming conversations when I have gotten off-track or stuck. After so many books, I tend to be a self-starter (and finisher) but every once in a while, I bring in someone else when a particular project is not moving along or I am unsure that I will get it done in a timely manner. Who could you use as an accountability partner? Do you need one? If so, who will you contact and by when? What, specifically, will you ask him or her to do?

WRITING COMMITMENTS AND PUBLISHING COMMITMENTS

There are also two areas in which writers typically make commitments or promises. One involves writing and the other involves completing steps to getting your writing published. I have found that knowing my books will get published gives me much more energy to write, so for me the two are intertwined.

✏️ **Writing Commitments Worksheet** ✏️

List five promises you will make about your writing. Remember to get specific about actions, timing, and results.

_____

_____

_____

_____

List five promises you will make about getting your writing out into the world and getting published. Remember to get specific about actions, timing, and results.

_____

_____

_____

_____

Writing commitments are concerned with anything that gets the book written: sitting down in front of the computer at a certain time of day or for a certain amount of time or reaching a certain word count. Publishing commitments are about anything that involves selling the book or getting it published. These are things like sending off three query letters to agents in the next week or hiring a freelance editor to polish your proposal by the end of the month.

Develop Writing Rituals

There was some research done years ago studying children who were surprisingly resilient in the face of difficult circumstances. The researchers studied kids who had one or both parents who were addicted to drugs or alcohol. These kids were often neglected, had undergone multiple traumas, and usually had unstable home environments. Many of them, as you might suspect, grew up to have a proclivity to crime, drug or alcohol problems, depression, and so on. But some did surprisingly well. They discovered that the kids who did better often had rituals that gave them some sort of stability amid the chaos of their lives. A grandmother read a story once a week; a boy went to a Boys' Club every day after school; a girl's dinnertime was always the same time and she sat at the same spot at the table.

In the same way, rituals can help writers by providing stability amid the stress of writing. By rituals, in this context, I mean regular habits or patterns (there are other kinds of rituals but we won't be dealing with them here). Developing rituals can help writers create a structure that helps them get their writing done and deal with the ups, downs, and challenges of the writing life. As with other suggestions in this book, feel free to pick and choose among these ideas. Whatever gets the book written and helps you be a better writer is the overarching consideration in this book.

I like to listen to loud rock music while I am writing. I am easily distractible and somehow this loud music feels like a bubble that surrounds me and helps me focus better. Getting the right music is important for me. It can't be music that is too new or I tend to stop writing and listen more closely to it. It has to be something I really like but am familiar enough with not to have to listen to it closely. It has to be coming through the speakers, not headphones, for some reason. Now, that ritual would probably not work for you or most of the people reading this. And that's the point of this section. I want to give you some ideas you might be able to spark off of to develop your own writing rituals.

PREWRITING RITUALS

What we call procrastination might well be incubation,
and the importance of prewriting—sorting things through,
assimilating, making connections.
—Henriette Anne Klauser

We'll discuss prewriting rituals first. Remember to distinguish between procrastinating avoidance maneuvers and things that actually help you get ready to write or write better and faster. Remember that the only person who will suffer is you if you fool yourself. Beginning writers (and even experienced ones) must be vigilant for those avoidant strategies that can weasel into the writing life. There are a million distractions that can derail your writing.

Having said that, some rituals can actually energize your writing or make it go better. I have found that when I don't take the time to outline my chapters well, the writing takes much more time and is not as good. So taking that time is not procrastination or avoidance, but actually moves the writing forward.

Inspiration rituals
How do you get inspired? How do you find the topic or theme of your book? How do you get inspired to write? When you

think about it, is there a pattern? If so, could you create a ritual to deliberately get inspired?

As I mentioned in an earlier chapter, different people have different energies that inform their writing: Some get blissed, excited about a topic or direction; others get pissed, angry, or upset about some area of life that motivates them to write.

I often develop my topics from teaching workshops. Someone in the audience asks a question that sparks a response I have never articulated before. Or I hear myself say something that is new or innovative. I occasionally stop and write down the idea because I have found that if I don't, it might be gone later. I even ask participants to give me a minute while I record it. Participants have told me that they don't mind this and are even proud to have been part of possibly seeding a new book.

Another way I get inspired is by hearing or reading other people with whom I disagree. My book *Thriving Through Crisis* was inspired when I heard a psychologist on CNN being interviewed on the one-year anniversary of the 9/11 attacks make this statement: "These people will never get over this. They will suffer from post-traumatic stress disorder the rest of their lives." I knew that he was wrong, both from my personal experience and from my knowledge of the research as a psychotherapist. I wanted to reach through that television screen and throttle him. Instead, my anger motivated me, and I wrote a proposal and sent it off to my agent. I should have gotten that psychologist's name and sent him a thank you note (along with a copy of the research studies that showed him how wrong his categorical statement had been).

A third inspiration ritual for me is going for a long car ride. One thing I like about long car rides is that my mind begins to wander after a few hundred miles and song lyrics, symphonies, plots for short stories, poems, article ideas, and book ideas appear unbidden in my mind. I have learned to bring a tape recorder with me to capture my ideas. When I am stuck with any part of a book, I can set my mind on that section and go for a long car ride, and that often helps me find new ideas and slants.

The final thing that works for me is swimming. My mind gets more fluid when I am in water, I guess, and for whatever reason, after about 10 minutes of swimming laps, I get all sorts of creative ideas. Of course, I have to remember them until I get out of the pool so that I can jot them down. I keep a small notebook and pen in my swim bag.

- What kinds of inspiration rituals can you come up with and try?
- What usually helps you be creative or inspired?

Getting ready to write rituals

Again, be vigilant not to use these rituals to avoid or put off writing. That said, writing rituals can help prepare you mentally to write and, by putting some parts of the writing process on automatic pilot, free the mind up to be creative or work more smoothly and easily in doing the writing.

Does it help you to be in a certain setting? What kind of atmosphere facilitates your writing or sticking to it? Do you need to have a certain chair set up, see the outdoors when you write, be around people, be alone, have it perfectly quiet? Or doesn't it matter?

The writer Malcolm Gladwell writes in coffeeshops. He was a journalist for years before going freelance and learned to write in a loud environment with others around. The coffeeshop is the closest he can get to that experience. Isabel Allende lights candles and meditates before she begins her novels.

Another issue writers have at times is setting boundaries. If you work at home, friends or family members sometimes think you are not really working or can stop at any time to do an errand, have a chat, do the laundry, or answer the phone. You might need to arrange the setting so they will get the message loud and clear. Put a stop sign on the door. Close the door. Set office hours and post them. Ask not to be disturbed unless it is an emergency when the sign is posted or the office hours are in effect.

Do you need to have boundaries around your online access so you don't fritter away your hours scanning profiles on Facebook, surfing the web, or compulsively checking email? The novelist Jonathan Franzen goes to an office with nothing in it but an old laptop on which he has disabled Internet access. He finds that helps him stay focused.

Again, this need for time and space boundaries is not universal. The thriller writer Steve Berry got so used to writing in small breaks during his workday as an attorney that if he retires from his practice, he jokes he will have to hire his secretary to interrupt him every 10 minutes. To have hours of uninterrupted writing time would be torture to him.

Are you more prepared to write when you are dressed, shaved, with makeup on? Or are you more in the mood to write in your underwear, bathrobe, and with bad hair and bad breath?

- What rituals do you go through to prepare yourself to write?
- Do you even have a ritual?
- Do you need one?

TOOLS

Again, don't use the lack of tools as a reason to put off writing, but sometimes the right tools really can make a difference. Would having that portable computer really help you write more or is it just another way of fooling yourself and procrastinating (and a justification for getting a new toy)?

- Do you like to use a special pen?
- A special kind of paper or notebook?

- A humongous dictionary?
- Do you need an online connection while you are writing?

The best-selling author James Patterson uses a pencil and sends his writing out to be typed. Then he corrects the ensuing triple-spaced manuscript with the same tool—a pencil. John Grisham is said to write on an old word processor that hasn't been upgraded in years.

TIMING RITUALS

Do you have or need particular ritualized times to write? Hours or days? Isabel Allende has always begun her books on the same day of the year (January 8th, the day she began her first novel, as a letter to her dying grandfather). Her unconscious, creative mind has gotten used to this timing and has been working on ideas before she sits down to write. Other writers use the same method but on a daily basis. Their unconscious knows they will be at the computer, typewriter, or writing desk at 9 a.m. every morning, so it begins to count on this ritual and prepare.

Other writers use timers. Some write in 5-minute bursts. Others write for 4 hours and call it quits, even if they are in the middle of a sentence or a great section. For other writers, awareness of time is unhelpful. One writer writes in a room with no outside view or light so he can't tell whether it is day or night or how much time has gone by. He has even gone so far as to put a bandage over the clock on his computer. The novelist Dan Brown begins his writing day at four in the morning, sets a timer, and every hour he gets up to stretch and do sit-ups and push-ups.

OUTLINING RITUALS

Joseph Wambaugh covers the walls, doors, and windows of his writing room with large pieces of butcher paper and begins to write notes and to Scotch-tape research clippings and notes in roughly chronological order when he is writing a nonfiction project. He says it looks like the scribblings of a demented person.

Here's a simple suggestion I use all the time. If I were going to teach a presentation on this topic, what are the main points I would like to include? Then I organize them into an outline for the proposed talk and, voilà, I have my book outline.

Or try telling your idea to someone else who has no knowledge of the subject but is an intelligent, good listener. Have him or her take notes on the main points he or she hears. Then go over it. If he or she has misunderstood, you haven't been clear. Go back and clarify the misunderstood points.

Some writers use "mind maps," graphical representations of their projects. Others outline longhand and linearly. Some take notes as they occur to them or as they research on three-by-five note cards and then rearrange those cards in some logical order. Some focus every waking moment on plotting or organizing the book, even while they are busy with everyday tasks. What works for you?

GETTING UNSTUCK/UNBLOCKED RITUALS

Dan Brown uses "gravity boots" and hangs upside down. He feels that the blood rushing to his head helps him figure his way out of stuck places when he is writing.

I read my writing aloud so I can hear where it stops flowing. This reading helps me generate new ideas as well. I also sit down and pretend that I am writing a letter to a good friend rather than writing a book. This informality helps me be less performance-oriented and I often discover what I truly want to say on the subject.

One author I know takes a long, hot bath. Another goes for a walk. Another does vigorous exercise like running or "spinning."

What rituals do you have to get unstuck or unblocked? If you don't have any, do you think it would be helpful to create or establish some? What would those be?

The daily count

Many full-time authors hold themselves to a daily word count: 1,000 words a day; 2,500 words a day. If this method appeals to you, you might work backward. This book was promised to be about 50,000 words. If I worked on it daily and committed to writing 1,000 words per day, I could get a draft done in 50 days. That would be just a couple of months, assuming I took a few days off. If I committed to 2,500 words per day, I could get the book draft done in 20 straight writing days. Just think, if you got up a few hours early each morning for a little less than a month, you could have the draft of your book done. When I am on a roll, I write 10,000 words a day, but I am a practiced and fast writer and I always work from a good outline and know my topic in and out before I start writing. Writing just 250 words per day (about a page) would get a book like this done in 200 days, less than a year. Think about it. If you wrote a page a day, you could have your book draft completed by this time next year. Wouldn't that be cool?

I have read that Stephen King writes every day, except on his birthday and Christmas. If he can do that, you can establish a daily habit and quota of words and start to get your writing done.

Get a Coauthor

James Patterson has cowritten several of his 34 novels. He says he has more ideas than time to write them. Tom Clancy farms out the writing of some of his novels based on ideas and characters he has created.

To get myself off the dime and to help me learn to write, I cowrote many of my early books (I write solo these days). I found the dialogue better than staring at a blank screen, and I figured I would learn something from my coauthors about how they wrote and their writing styles.

Sometimes my choice of coauthor has been a disaster. I have ended up doing most of the work but still share royalties and credit. It turned out to be more work than it would have been if I had just written the book by myself. But, other times, it's been a delight: both the process and the outcome. One coauthor, Michele Weiner-Davis, and I spent much of our cowriting time laughing. Despite that, we eventually got the book finished. It is still in print almost 25 years later. Other times, the coauthor's writing and contribution to the project were fine, but getting him or her to do the right share of the work was like pulling teeth.

I have another coauthor, Bob Bertolino, with whom I have created five books, and he is much better at details than I am. If I can't find a reference as the editing process comes to a close, I am likely to throw out the sentence or paragraph. Bob is willing to search to the ends of the earth to find the missing reference. So that leads to another suggestion for finding and working with coauthors: Find one who has complementary skills. If you are good with dialogue but not plotting, find someone with that strength. If you are good at outlining, but terrible at details, find someone who is detail-oriented.

That leads to another suggestion: Try a small project or a trial period of cowriting with someone before you commit to a book or bigger project. Like any other relationship in life, coauthors can be heaven or hell. Good coauthorship, like great friendships or marriages, hinges mainly on compatibility and regular clear communication.

I wouldn't have nearly as many books out now if I hadn't had coauthors at a crucial period of time in my development as a writer. Consider this option to get your book written.

Speak Your Book

In my early years as an author, writing was difficult for me, but by then, I had developed my confidence and abilities as a public speaker by giving two or three talks per month. I found speaking as easy as falling off a log.

Someone suggested that I begin recording my workshops and transcribing them to create books. I thought it was a good idea. I tried it for the first time with my book *Solution-Oriented Hypnosis*. I had someone record it, paid someone to transcribe it, and sat down to edit it. I discovered it was harder than writing a book from scratch. I found, to my chagrin, that I regularly spoke in ungrammatical sentences, skipped around between thoughts, didn't finish thoughts, and so on. It took me a bit longer to finish that book than usual because it involved so much editing. But the book was different, more lively, than all my other books. Readers who had been to my workshops told me that it vividly evoked my speaking style and was easy to read.

I tried the method again some years later with another book project and found it was much easier and went more smoothly. This time I didn't record a workshop. I just stood (I had to stand to get the energy and feeling right) in my office and recorded what I wanted to say. The book was completed a bit quicker than my usual writing project and came out well. Again, like most writing projects, don't try and wing it. Have a solid detailed outline from which to work before you try to speak your book.

So, if you are more glib and articulate when speaking rather than writing, you might try this out. With transcription software on computers becoming more accurate, you might even be able to skip paying someone to transcribe it.

COMPLETING YOUR BOOK

Getting yourself to write is one thing, but getting yourself to complete a book project is another. Seth Godin, a marketing professional, talks about the importance of having a "ship date." When he worked at software companies, the software engineers wanted to work on the code ad infinitum, tweaking, adding more features, fixing little bugs. Finally, the boss would put his foot down and declare a "ship date," which was the date the software had to be released to the world. Having such a completion date focused everyone. In the last days before shipping, people worked hard to complete the product.

Believe me, in general in my life, I can be the king of procrastination and avoidance. But somehow I have found a way to overcome that tendency when it comes to my books. I have been able to do it in several ways. First, as we discussed in the first chapter, I needed to identify and tap into the energy that propelled me to write. This, for me, was a combination of blissed and pissed. I was passionate about communicating certain ideas and methods to my colleagues and later to the general public that I thought were really cool and could help relieve suffering in the world. I was also upset about what I saw as the intractable discouragement and negative focus of a good percentage of my psychotherapy colleagues. I felt called and compelled to change my field so that it served clients better.

Next, because most of my books have been produced by traditional print publishers, I always had some money up front and a contract that specified a date on which the manuscript was to be turned in. I mentioned this before, but I almost always keep my promises to others, especially when there is money and a contract involved.

I often intend to do various projects—clean out the garage, exercise regularly, self-publish a book—that I don't stick to or pin myself down to a due date. Having that external accountability has helped me overcome my tendency to let things slide or to think that I'll get to it later. Now, having completed about 30 traditionally published books, I can more readily keep my intentions with self-published projects, having exercised the muscle of both writing and keeping a publishing deadline.

Here are some words from another coauthor of one of my previous books, Sandy Beadle, about a strategy she used to write one of her books:

I have been struggling with bookus interruptus for years. My next book got waylaid when the energy was still there, the energy went away, it has taken far too long, and I really lost focus.

I know that there's nothing like a deadline to get me focused, so I asked someone in my seminar if I could send her a page or a chapter every week. She did not have to comment, or even read it—just catch it.

That was 83 weeks ago, and I just mailed my 79th file to her. Sometimes it's just a paragraph, once it was a picture, sometimes it's a whole chapter. I recently told her I was going to arbitrarily call it finished when I got to 100 items, so that is not far off.

Can you find a way to create a ship date for each section of your book and for the book in general? One that matters? One that will get you to stick to it?

Find a Writing Accountability Partner

If you don't have a book contract or a ship date that will get you to write and complete your book project, then consider getting yourself an accountability partner. This is a friend, a family member, a coach, a colleague, or anyone you can enlist (or pay) to help you keep your word and get your writing done.

I'm not talking about finding someone to lay a guilt trip on you; you just need someone to remind you of your best intentions and work with you to keep your writing commitments.

First, get really clear on a realistic plan for getting your writing done. Then find your accountability partner and make a clear schedule for him or her to check in with you or vice versa (or both) on certain milestones or due dates. It might be daily, weekly, monthly, or just on particular days. It could be by email, by phone, by Skype, or in person. Make sure you choose a person who won't be pulled in by your excuses but who will calmly remind you of what you said you would do and when you said you would do it.

THE ZEN OF WRITING

*It's amazing how long it takes to complete something
you're not working on.*

—R. D. Clyde

Early in my career, I worked for a drug and alcohol treatment center. One day I had a blinding revelation that was so simple and so profound that it really clarified things for me. I realized that the only way to stop drinking was to stop putting alcohol in one's mouth and swallowing it. That's it. Everything else was theory, conjecture, explanation, systems.

After this long chapter in which I have given you all these possibilities for getting your book written, here is the bottom line, the Zen simple truth of the matter. *The only way to get your book written is to sit down and write it* (or stand up if you prefer; you know what I mean). That's it. This leads to the principle of the Zen of writing: The only way to write is to write. All the rest is commentary, procrastination, reasons why you don't have time or can't write, and so on. All that is NOT WRITING.

So, instead of trying to work out how you will write, sit down and write. You'll find much more writing goes on when you move out of thinking about writing and into actual writing. This seems obvious, but you'd be surprised at how much time and how many convolutions people go through instead of just sitting down and writing.

When I first got the notion to write, I knew something about myself that might stop me. I have a tendency to procrastinate and to think about doing things rather than doing them. Because I was determined to get my ideas out in book form (I wasn't actually excited about writing like some of you may be), I decided then and there that I would skip reading books about writing or going to writers' conferences or anything else that didn't involve actual writing. I must tell you that this made the process of writing much more difficult and resulted in lots of bad writing, but at least I finished my books. I think that there is a lot to learn from reading books about how to write, how to get yourself to write, how to write well, and how to sell your work. Writers' conferences are good places to get a sense of the field, to meet others in writing and publishing, and sometimes to help sell your work. But, for me, there were dangerous traps in those activities. I knew that I was likely to do them instead of writing.

Bryce Courtenay, an Australian author of many books, including *The Power of One*, put it this way when asked how he wrote so much: bum glue. He sits his butt down and writes. Even if you write standing up or dictating, you get the point: Do it. Bryce says that because he didn't start writing until he was in his 50s and he has so many books to write, he writes eight months of the year and works 12 hours a day, 6 days a week until he finishes a book. Howard Fast has a similar take: *How did I become a writer? That can be answered in one line—the back of my seat to the seat of the chair.* I heard that in his early writing days the author John McPhee tied the sash of his bathrobe to his chair to keep himself from leaving it.

A friend of mine, Dennis Palumbo, a former screenwriter turned therapist, has a principle that puts it another way: *Writing begets writing; not writing begets not writing.* He recommends that if you don't know what to write about or you don't feel like writing, sit down and write about not knowing what to write about or about not feeling like writing. Inertia will tend to take you in the direction you are already going. If you are writing, you tend to write more. If you are not writing, you tend not to write. Dorianne Laux says something similar: *There is so much about the process of writing that is myste-rious to me, but this one thing I've found to be true: Writing begets writing.*

Sinclair Lewis once spoke to some students about being a writer. He asked them, "How many of you here are really serious about being writers?" Lots of hands went up. Lewis asked, "Well, why aren't you all home writing?" and he walked out of the classroom. A dramatic example, but I think he made his point.

On that same theme, Ray Bradbury once lectured at a creative writing class and was asked, "Mr. Bradbury, you are so productive. You've written many short stories, books, screenplays, and so on. How do you get in the mood to write? Sometimes I'm just not in the mood." Bradbury looked over his big white bushy eyebrows at the student and replied, "Sit down and write, son. It will take care of all those moods you are having."

Joyce Carol Oates gives much the same advice: "One must be pitiless about this matter of 'mood.' In a sense, the writing will create the mood. . . . I have forced myself to begin writing when I've been utterly exhausted, when I've felt my soul as thin as a playing card, when nothing seemed worth enduring for another five minutes . . . and somehow the activity of writing changes everything."

Your task as a writer is to write. Imagine if you were a plumber and you went to a customer's house to fix the pipes. Would you tell him that you were afraid of failure so you were not really ready to work yet? Or wait for the house to be completely quiet, with no distractions? Or that you had "plumber's block" and didn't really know how to proceed? Or would you sit for hours trying to work out a strategy for approaching the pipes in an optimum way? No, you would think about it a little and then dive right in, working out the problems you encountered as you went.

It's the same thing with writing. Dive right in. There are sure to be some snags along the way, but you probably won't know what they are until you get to them. So get to them by writing.

And disregard your feelings. As a therapist, I love to say this to other therapists. When it's time to write, *don't get in touch with your feelings; don't go with your feelings.* Your feelings will usually be telling you that you can't write or that you are too afraid or it's not the right time or some other such claptrap. Thank those feelings for sharing and get on with it. Ignore them. Tune them out and get those fingers typing or writing. Don't wait for inspiration or the muse to visit. J. B. Priestly advises that "perhaps it would be better not to be a writer, but if you must, then write. If it all feels hopeless, if that famous 'inspiration' will not come, write. If you are a genius, you'll make your own rules, but if not—and the odds are against it—go to your desk, no matter what your mood, face the icy challenge of the paper—write."

Are you getting the point I am hammering in yet? Writers who complete projects write. Sure, they have rituals and tricks and struggles. But in the end, they do the work. They write no matter what else is going on within them or in the world. They carve out time from busy lives to write. And they keep writing until they complete something.

How Do I Not Write? Let Me Count the Ways

Let's keep this pretty simple. Almost anything you do that doesn't involve getting words down is you avoiding or procrastinating (with very few exceptions). Sure, there is a certain amount of preparation, outlining, or research that is usually done before writing, but after that, it's time to write. Some people think long and hard about their words before actually putting them on the screen or paper, but for most of us, thinking about writing is what we do not to write. As David Long admonishes: *You can't sit around thinking. You have to sit around writing.*

We all have our own avoidance habits. For my first several books, I had to let my magazine subscriptions lapse for the duration of the writing project. If a magazine was in the house, it had an almost magnetic allure for me. I could avoid reading books, because they were clearly going to take up large chunks of time, but a little magazine with bite-sized articles? Surely that would be okay. The trouble is that I would pick one up and be busy for hours. Because I was working full time and raising four kids at the time, there went my potential writing time. These days I get sucked in by the Internet or iPad games.

What is the magnet for your avoidance or procrastination? What do you do rather than write?

Here is a list of common avoidance or procrastination tasks I have used or heard about from others:

Sharpen your pencils.
Buy new pens.
Clean up your office or writing space.
Talk to others about what you will write.
Think about writing.
Read about writing.
Go to writers' conferences.
Obsess about why you aren't writing.
Find reasons why you aren't writing.
Worry about success, failure, or critics.
Talk to your therapist about your writer's block or why you
    are sabotaging yourself.
Buy and install new software.
Get a new computer.
Check your email.
Surf the 'net.
Watch television.
Read books, magazines, or newspapers.

It's time to take an honest inventory of your preferred or typical ways of not writing. No one else really knows what belongs on this list but you. And you can always fool yourself or others. So, without being unnecessarily harsh with yourself, honestly admit what you do to avoid or procrastinate. Then when you notice yourself doing one or more of these things, you can instantly apply the magical antidote: START WRITING!

In fact, you might even link these things to make them cues for writing. Every time you discover one of your nonwriting habits popping up, the next time you notice yourself doing it, sit down and write for 5 minutes (or longer). That way, you will begin to train yourself out of those nonwriting habits and into writing.

Make a list of things you typically do other than writing:

1.

2.

3.

4.

5.

6.

7.

8.

9.

10.

(Continue on a piece of paper if you need more room; and God help you.)

Now choose the most time-sucking items on the list from which you don't really derive that much benefit; the "empty calories" of your activities. And then make a "NOT TO-DO" list. Place a reminder in a prominent place, someplace you will see it regularly, such as the bathroom mirror. Remind yourself of what you are not going to do in order to get your writing done.

CHECKLIST FOR ESSENTIAL FIRST STEPS TOWARD WRITING YOUR BOOK

- Set a due date for having a certain amount of writing done and having the whole writing project done.
- Start writing in small increments, 5 minutes per day at least.
- Discover your best method of getting your writing done.
- Find an accountability partner and set times/dates for check-ins.
- Have a plan for getting back on track if you get derailed.
- Find an editor or editors to give you corrections and feedback.
- Persist until your book is completed.
- Writing begets writing; don't wait to be in the right mood or until you feel like writing; sit down and write.

CHECKLIST FOR NEXT STEPS TO GETTING YOUR BOOK PUBLISHED

- Create a working outline/chapter list for your book.
- Begin to find, attract, and connect to your niche audience (through blogs, teleseminars, speaking, networking, article writing, podcasts, pay-per-click ads, social media, free giveaways in exchange for email addresses, etc.).
- Begin planning or expanding your web presence (a book-related or niche-related domain name choice and purchase, blog, website, email list, etc.).
- Research your niche keywords.
- Line up some technical help to implement web and email tasks.
- Start writing in small increments (5 minutes; 1,000 words) on a regular basis.

CHAPTER 5

If You Build It, They May Not Come
Carving a Platform to Help Sell Your Book

SOMETIMES YOU MAY WONDER WHY some therapists get their books published when your ideas are just as good as theirs (or better). Well, it's because who gets published is not just a matter of who has the best ideas. It's also influenced by who can sell books and how well known the author is.

I know it can seem like a catch-22. How do you get well known without a book? Most of the best-known therapists have written at least one book. Often they have written more then one.

So, let me tell you a couple of stories that will help you understand the publishing buzzword and important element that will help you get your book (or books) published. It's called the platform.

Some years ago, I traveled to New York to make the rounds of some big publishers who were potentially interested in buying my next book. My literary agent accompanied me on these visits and the scene was almost identical at each publishing house. We would be ushered into a conference room and seated at a large table with several employees of the publishing house, usually the editor who was considering acquiring my book, a marketing person, perhaps the executive editor, and a secretary to take notes. After we had all gotten our coffees or waters and met each other, the editor would lead with, "Bill, we agreed to meet with you and consider your proposal because we love your platform. You have a really big platform." I would nod as if I understood, but I really wasn't sure what this jargon word meant.

After hearing this same phrase in several meetings, I asked my agent exactly what "platform" meant and she explained it was essentially one's credibility and reputation. It was constructed of things like whether one was perceived as a thought leader or an expert by one's peers or whether one had published in peer-reviewed journals.

I later learned that that is only part of what people in the publishing field call "platform"; in this chapter, I will break down the components of it, tell you why it is so crucial to your publishing success, and explain how to articulate and expand your platform to make it more likely you will get your book published.

And that leads to my second story. Before I had published any books, I volunteered to edit the Milton H. Erickson Foundation Newsletter. I had previously edited the NLP Newsletter and when Jeff Zeig and I, both students of the late Dr. Erickson, met up in 1981, he suggested I start up and edit a newsletter for the newly founded Milton H. Erickson Foundation.

I had also begun teaching workshops on Dr. Erickson's work and was eager to get the word out about them, so I started a Workshop Listing section in the newsletter. That helped get me a bit of a reputation and led to an invitation to teach my first international workshops, because someone in England subscribed to the Erickson newsletter, liked my workshop titles, and invited me to teach a series of workshops there.

After editing the newsletter for a few years, I was attending a large psychotherapy conference when I received a call in my hotel room from Seymour Weingarten, the executive editor of a psychotherapy publisher named Guilford. Seymour asked me to meet him for drinks and a chat and said Jeff Zeig had told him that I knew everyone who was anyone in the Erickson field. (And indeed I did; I was obsessed with Erickson's work and my role as the newsletter editor put me at the hub of the latest information in that area.)

When we met, Seymour explained that his publishing company was behind the competition in the Ericksonian area, which was exploding in popularity at the time. Could I tell him who the hot new Ericksonian experts were who hadn't yet written books that Guilford might snag? I gave him a rundown on those folks and then, immodestly, mentioned that I had plans to write some books (I had five outlined in my head, actually). He asked about my books and by the end of the conversation, to my astonishment, we had made a handshake deal that he would publish one of those five.

I walked away from that conversation very excited and holding a mystical "law of attraction" kind of sense that I had made my dreams come true just by wishing for them. I realized much later that although my intentions didn't hurt, they were not the main factor in scoring this coup. It was my platform. What do I mean? At the time I met with Seymour, I was leading two or three workshops per month all around the United States and occasionally in other countries. I was the editor of a widely read newsletter in the field. I gave presentations at large conferences with several thousand attendees.

Think of it from the publisher's point of view. He could give a book contract to a professor at a university (who had a more prestigious degree and academic qualifications than I had), but how many people could that professor alert about the book and how many could that professor motivate to buy the book? Probably several hundred students and fellow faculty.

How many could I? Perhaps 10,000+ every year. If even 15% of those people bought my book, I could sell 1,500 books per year and that would continue for the life of the

book. If another several thousand saw notice of it in the newsletter I edited, it could sell another 1,000 or more (because
the readers were my prime audience). Perhaps the law of
attraction was working, but my guess is that the publisher saw
the law of marketing and numbers working more reliably and
so he took the risk to sign me up. And that is platform.

The platform is your ability to find an audience for your
book and let them know that it is available. It is a combination
of your reputation, your credibility, your marketing abilities,
and your marketing channels and how you can reach readers
now and in the future. It is your portfolio, just like that big
briefcase of artworks and slides that artists bring around to
show gallery owners.

In addition to the quality of the idea behind your book and
the quality of the writing, the platform is the biggest factor in
a book's success. And it is something that you can control in
two ways:

1. How well you articulate your current platform
2. How much you expand your platform between the time
   you read this and when you begin to sell your book

THE PLANKS OF YOUR PLATFORM

Think of a platform as literally a stage, a riser, that could lift
you up above the crowd.

If a publisher walked into a room with thousands of would-
be authors, it could be a little overwhelming, especially if that
publisher was busy and didn't have time to personally get to
know each of these authors and find out in detail about their
book ideas.

If one of those authors in the crowded room, however, had
found a stage or platform on which to stand, he or she would
naturally stand out from the crowd and be easier to spot.

The publisher would notice him or her and be more likely to choose that author to get to know.

So your platform is built plank by plank until it becomes high enough for publishers to consider your book project and for readers to notice you and your book above all the others that are coming out daily and weekly. What are the planks, the components, of a platform? I have created an acronym, CARVE, to help articulate the components and make them more memorable. You can carve your platform out of these five elements.

C=Connections
A=Accomplishments
R=Reputation
V=Visibility
E=Evidence

C Is for Connections

Remember how I mentioned that Jeff Zeig suggested I start the Milton Erickson Foundation Newsletter and also that Seymour Weingarten then wanted to meet with me? *Connections*. I got to know Jeff Zeig because we were both students of Milton Erickson. *Connections*. I got to know Milton Erickson because I met him when he visited the art gallery where I worked at Arizona State University. Then I wrote him a letter and he invited me to study with him. *Connections*.

Of course, not everything happens through connections (that's why there are five elements in carving your platform), but connections can be important and, in some cases, crucial.

Do you know anyone who might know an agent you could approach (if you need an agent)? Who could help make your work or book more visible? Who could help you develop your reputation and credibility? Do you have social media sites on which you develop and expand your connections?

Seth Godin talks about finding your "tribe," that set of like-minded people interested in and passionate about the topic in which you are interested. If you can become a well-known person or well connected in that community, you would be carving part of your platform: the connections part.

A Is for Accomplishments

Jeff Zeig wouldn't have thought of me as a potential editor of the Erickson Foundation Newsletter unless I had previously edited a newsletter. I started the NLP Newsletter because I was interested in neurolinguistic programming (NLP) and I was frustrated that there was no central source of news and training opportunities.

No one gave me permission (or funding) to start that newsletter. I just went ahead and did it. Of course, I never imagined that it would lead to anything other than itself, but now that I have been around for a while, I have realized that anything one accomplishes in life gives one credibility, visibility, experience, and expertise, and these bonuses often lead to relationships and connections.

So your task is to document your accomplishments in general and more particularly in the niche area related to your book topic. And then get to work creating more accomplishments in that area before you submit your book to an editor, agent, or publisher.

R Is for Reputation

Obviously there is some overlap among the components I have listed here that make up one's platform, and one can easily recognize this when it comes to reputation.

One's reputation is made up of what people think or know about you (connections) and what you have accomplished (as well as how nice a person you are, how reliable you are, how easy to work with you are, how well you keep your word, etc.).

I have never delivered a manuscript late to a publisher. That is part of my reputation. I am generally easygoing and easy to get along with. That is another part of my reputation.

I had a coauthor some years ago who was constantly in crisis (financial, relational, medical), and he delayed delivering his part of a joint project for quite a while. Each time he would delay, I would receive a letter (this was in the days before faxes and emails, young'uns, and, no, the letters weren't delivered by postmen on dinosaurs).

My then wife and I would have fun holding up the latest unopened letter from this man and guessing which crisis *du jour* it would be this time. We were sometimes wrong on the particulars but always spot on about the fact that it was another crisis and an excuse for another delay. That is reputation.

Of course, you want to create a reputation of being a capable, trustworthy person who is easy to work with and who will deliver the goods.

V Is for Visibility

For people to find your book, it (and perhaps you) must be visible. The more visible your book is in as many places and in as many ways as possible, the better.

Some books have a new life when they get made into movies. Why? Because those books are more visible (more people go to movies than read books, or at least a different group of people goes to movies and that ups the visibility of the book).

Getting your book discussed through the mass media often boosts sales. My best-selling book to date was the one featured on *Oprah*. It continues to sell well 13 years after this episode, in part because visibility leads to more visibility. Because it sold well, somebody may see it on a friend's bookshelf. Or because it was featured on the Oprah website, someone may come across it there. When I speak, the organizers often make sure that book, *Do One Thing Different*, is for sale at the back of the room or the conference bookstore. Radio exposure is good as well, as is a review in a national newspaper.

But with the existence of the Internet, it has become easier for authors to make their books more visible. You could start a blog based on your book. You could put up a website inexpensively and quickly with the book's title as the web address. You could create YouTube videos featuring the book or related material with a link back to your website or blog or to your book being sold through an online bookseller. Some authors are doing "blog book tours" or "virtual book tours," where they are interviewed by other bloggers or podcasters about their book in a written form, an audio form, or even via video or Skype.

And, just to be clear on visibility, there are two ways to make your book more visible. One is to become more visible yourself: Find your audience, find your tribe, get followers in general. Then use that visibility to make your book visible. The other is to just focus on making the book more visible. Either will work. But if you plan to publish more than one book, your constant task should be to make yourself more visible.

Some people feel a bit uncomfortable putting themselves or their work forward. Just think of it as getting the contribution you have to make in front of the people to whom you could be of service. If they never find out about it, they can never get the help your work may provide for them.

E Is for Evidence

All the assertions in the world about the size and power of your platform don't matter much if you can't provide evidence for it. Publishers have gotten burned so much by overly ambitious people with a tenuous grip on truth (can you say *A Million Little Pieces*?) that they want evidence of your platform before they will believe it exists.

Your task, therefore, is to gather all the evidence you can of your visibility, the size of your audience, any blurbs you have gotten, your TV and radio appearances, and so on, to be able to show you are telling the truth.

Anything that shows your credibility, your accomplishments, your visibility, your media presence or appearances, your online and social media presence and followers or connections, your marketing abilities, and your reputation should be documented in written form, an audio, a video, or screenshots.

A screenshot, for those of you who don't know, is a picture you take of your computer screen. For example, when I visit my email list management service and look up the size of my email list (about 7,000 at the time of this writing), I can take a picture of that number to show that I am not lying or making it up.

PLATFORM AND SELF-PUBLISHING

Your platform is crucial if you are seeking a contract with a traditional print publisher (more crucial if you are writing a "trade" book that needs an agent), but here's the thing: Even if you are planning to self-publish your book, the platform is important. Why? Because you need a good-sized platform to find readers and move them to buy your book.

Platform Envy

Once, when I was leading a boot camp on writing and publishing, one of the participants proclaimed that after learning about platform and hearing about the 20-some books I had published and my busy speaking schedule, he had developed a case of "platform envy." He was discouraged by realizing he didn't have much of a platform compared to mine.

I could feel the same way when I think about Stephen King or Deepak Chopra, but the point is not to get discouraged. Instead, work on expanding your platform starting exactly where you are.

That participant was Bill Sununu and, after his comment about platform envy, we worked together to put together his platform statement. He went home and worked on it more after the boot camp ended. What he came up with blew my mind and gave me a touch of platform envy in return. To put what you are about to read in context, Bill was working as a US Airways flight attendant and was also a social worker. As you read this next part, you might keep a running total of all the people Bill can let know about his book when it is published. His platform helped him get his first book published and garnered him a pretty good advance.

Here is his platform statement:

I can utilize my own extensive contacts to publicize the book. For example:

1. The Association of Flight Attendants (AFA) has already agreed to endorse the book. AFA sends out emails to over 40,000 flight attendants weekly and will include a press release on the book within its weekly message. The leadership of AFA is supportive of my endeavors and familiar with my work through the Pegasus Project. (The Pegasus Project is a non-profit organization, under the umbrella of AFA, that counsels and assists terminally ill and critically injured flight attendants. I have been a board member of the Pegasus Project for many years.)
2. John McCorkle, a well-known airline analyst, has agreed to issue a press release through his email subscription, the John McCorkle Newsletter. This national update on the airline industry goes out to over 12,000 journalists, stock analysts, airline management, and employees bi-monthly.
3. I have the support and endorsement of US Airways management. Crew Communication Supervisor Peter

Pellegrino has agreed to put a press release into CBS, the Crew Broadcasting System for US Airways crew members, which will go directly to 8,000 US Airways flight attendants and 4,000 pilots. In addition, I can get press releases placed in both American Airlines and United Airlines flight attendant emails that will reach an additional 38,000 individuals. Finally, Chris Collins, a vice president with JetBlue, has endorsed my book and will set up a book signing for JetBlue employees at Kennedy Airport.

4. Due to my personal contacts in the airline industry, volunteer associations, and international connections, I can send notices about the book to more than 2,000 colleagues and associates. In addition, I have the support of my cousin, John E. Sununu, the U.S. Senator, and my uncle, John Sununu, the former governor of New Hampshire and the chief of staff of the Bush Administration, in making this book a success.

5. I will contact the alumni associations of my alma maters, the American School of Athens, Greece; Purdue University; and the University of Chicago, and forward each of them a press release to place in their alumni publications, which together reach 900,000 people.

Okay, if you were keeping tabs, that adds up to more than a million people he can tell about his book. If even 1% of those people buy his book, he would sell 10,000 copies. That is more than respectable for a first-time, unknown author.

Bill did well enough with his first book to get a contract for his next and to begin to get speaking engagements. (Check out his first book, *Life Could Be Sweeter*.)

The point for you? Instead of collapsing in discouragement because other people are more well known than you are right now or have better marketing channels or abilities, get to work building your own platform. It is easier and less expensive than ever to build a platform.

Getting Blurbs From Well-Known People

Some time ago, I taught a workshop in Texas, and a participant came up and chatted with me. His name stuck with
me because it was Newton Hightower and I had read some
columns by a Texas political commentator named Jim Hightower. About a year after that encounter, I received a package
in the mail with Newton Hightower's forthcoming book (*Anger
Busting 101*), with a note reminding me of our meeting and
asking me for a blurb (endorsement) for the book.

Now I get hundreds of requests for book blurbs per year,
some from very good friends, and if I were to read all the
books and then spend time creating and sending blurbs, I
would barely have enough time to write any of my own books,
much less make a living or have a personal life. So I usually
say no. But even though I didn't know Newton Hightower
personally, I instantly gave him a blurb. Why?

Because he made it so easy and quick I could barely
refuse. He kindly summarized his book in a few pages,
included a copy so I could read more in-depth if I wanted, and
gave me several pages of potential blurbs he had prewritten
for me. I only had to circle the one I wanted to use and fax it
back to him. He had his blurb within an hour after I opened
his package.

I did something similar for one of my first books. I came
up with a blurb I thought would be great and then asked a
professional colleague if he would say that about my book. He
readily agreed and I had my blurb. (In case you are curious,
the blurb was *Warning: Reading this book could be hazardous
to your cherished beliefs and assumptions.*) But Newton
Hightower had gone one step further. He had given me many
blurbs from which to choose *and* he had summarized the
book.

People who are famous are often busy. When asked to
participate in a research project being done by the psycholo-

gist Mihaly Csikszentmihalyi, the management consultant and author Peter Drucker gave this reply: "I am greatly honored and flattered by your kind letter of February 14th—for I have admired you and your work for many years, and I have learned much from it. But, my dear Professor Csikszentmih- alyi, I am afraid I have to disappoint you. I could not possibly answer your questions. I am told I am creative—I don't know what that means. . . . I just keep on plodding. . . . I hope you will not think me presumptuous or rude if I say that one of the secrets of productivity (in which I believe whereas I do not believe in creativity) is to have a VERY BIG waste paper basket to take care of ALL invitations such as yours—productivity in my experience consists of NOT doing anything that helps the work of other people but to spend all one's time on the work the Good Lord has fitted one to do, and to do well."

I feel the same way and so do many productive and accomplished people. But I dare to say that Drucker may have been more inclined to give a blurb if he were asked in the way Newton Hightower approached me.

I'll give you one other pep talk and hint about getting blurbs from well-known people. This comes from my expe- rience with the psychologist Steven Wolinsky. Steven had organized a workshop to bring me down to Santa Fe where he lived. As he drove me to the airport, he placed a large brown- paper-wrapped bundle in my hands and asked me for a blurb for his just-completed book.

I read it on the way home and found it to be a mess. I reluctantly wrote him and told him the book needed to be edited and rewritten before I would even consider giving a blurb. I didn't hear a word back from him for a year (and never got another invitation to Santa Fe from him either), and I figured he had been offended by my response.

But a year later, though, another version of the book arrived via mail and this time, it was significantly improved (he had hired a professional editor). I sent him a blurb and a letter of congratulations. The printed book arrived in the mail a few months later and it had blurbs by me and Ernest Rossi, another of Milton Erickson's students.

A year later, I received another manuscript from Steven and gave him another blurb. This time when I received the printed book, it had endorsements by me, Rossi, and also John Bradshaw, who was a very well-known speaker, author, and TV show presenter at the time. I was impressed just to be on the same cover with Bradshaw.

The next year, I didn't receive a manuscript, but only Steven's next printed book, this time with endorsements from Bradshaw and also Albert Ellis, one of the most prominent psychotherapists in the world. I figured he no longer needed my endorsement because these others carried so much weight. But I wondered how he had obtained blurbs from such prominent and busy people. I called him up and he told me he had simply called each of them on the phone and asked for a blurb. I told him I would never have the nerve to do that.

Steven was deeply into Eastern religions and had studied for years in India with a guru. He had come to believe that the whole universe was an illusion and that we were all God playing at not being God by hiding in our individual identities. He said that since he deeply believed this version of reality, calling Albert Ellis or John Bradshaw on the phone was merely himself talking to himself in another form, so why should he be intimidated?

I got his point, but I would still find it intimidating to call them. But, even without Steven's unusual perspective, think about it. What's the worst that could happen? The famous person could turn you down or be rude or upset about the request. While unpleasant for a few moments, perhaps, the risk and pain compared to the reward of getting a blurb from such a well-known person are pretty insignificant in the grand scheme of things.

Go for it.

Start Small and Expand

Remember how I started with the NLP Newsletter, then moved on to the Milton Erickson Foundation Newsletter? The first was something I started on my own, but it led to a position with a larger institution. I had started small and on my own, and the attention, visibility, and credibility from that first small project had led to something bigger. From that Erickson Newsletter came my first international workshops.

I started small with my writing as well. First, I wrote some articles in a journal I edited. Then a few psychotherapy books, which are much easier to get published than books for the general public that need agents. Then I got an agent and got a few of those general-public books published. One of them got me on Oprah.

We sometimes look at well-known and accomplished people and think they are just lucky or that they were somehow always famous. But mostly they built their platform one plank at a time to get where they are today.

So start small, but start. Do whatever you can to build your platform and expand it between now and when your book is published. On the next page is a worksheet for you to articulate and expand your platform.

✏️ The Platform Worksheet ✏️

These are the elements of my platform:

❏ Previous media appearances

❏ Books or other previous publications

❏ Presentations/talks given

❏ Scheduled public speaking events in the future

❏ Great feedback comments from talks

❏ Blurbs from well-known or credible experts in my area

❏ Research I have done or that I have compiled

❏ Statistics on the size and motivation of my audience/readers

❏ Snail-mail mailing-list size

❏ Marketing avenues available

❏ Marketing experience

❏ Advertising/PR I have done or will do

❏ Degree

❏ Toll-free telephone number

❏ Publicity/marketing plan for this book

❏ Email newsletter and mailing-list size

❏ Website and large number of visitors or hits

❏ Blog

❏ YouTube Channel and number of views

❏ Facebook business page

❏ LinkedIn account and number of connections

❏ Twitter account and number of Twitter followers

❏ Any other social media accounts and influence

❏ Media coaching I have had

❏ Google ranking for me or my topic

❏ Sales results from previous books or products

❏ Professional materials for my business (letterhead, logo, etc.) and proposal

continued on following page

I think I need to add the following details:

The first step I plan to take to expand my platform is:

I plan to take this step by:

Other steps I plan to take or material I need to gather:

✏️ Platform Commitment and Tracking Worksheet ✏️

Now the rubber hits the road. Please use this Platform Commitment and Tracking Worksheet.

What are you going to do between now and when you go to sell your book or publish your book to articulate and expand your platform?

By when will you do these things you plan to do?

How will you keep yourself on track with these commitments and tasks? How will you get yourself back on track if you get sidetracked or derailed?

Do you need a partner or coach to help you get clear on what you will do and stay on track? Someone to help hold you accountable?

CHAPTER 6

Planning
Well Begun Is Half Done

WHEN PEOPLE MEET ME, they are sometimes surprised that I have written and published so many books. You see, I am naturally a bit disorganized and distractible. How do I write my books, then? Planning helps a great deal.

Of course, having signed a contract with a publisher, as I have with most of my books, builds in a little planning. The contract specifies a due date for the book. Because I have had to create a proposal with a chapter outline, the content is somewhat planned in advance as well (although the outline often changes, a little or a lot, during the actual writing).

I have also had to pre-think and plan who the audience is for the book and what the focus of the book is. But, other than that, it is generally up to me to organize myself to get the book written and delivered on time. I have discovered that the more planning I do ahead of time, the faster and more smoothly the writing and selling of the book goes.

OUTLINING

I make a very tight outline of everything I write before I write it. . . . By writing an outline you really are writing in a way, because you're creating the structure of what you're going to do. Once I really know what I'm going to write, I don't find the actual writing takes all that long.

—Tom Wolfe

I generally start a book with three things: (1) the original spark of an idea and passion for the book; (2) a title (not always, but sometimes I have a title early on); and (3) an outline.

If I don't do an outline, I am not certain it can be a book. It could just be an article or merely a good idea. Doing an outline reassures me I have the possibility of an actual book. I happen to be blessed with an outline mind. I find outlining relatively quick and easy. And you may be the same. But if this isn't your strong suit, here are some suggestions for creating your book outline.

Here's a simple idea I use all the time for myself. If I were going to teach a presentation on this topic, what are the main points I would like to include? Then I organize them into an outline for the proposed talk and voilà, I have my book outline.

Here's another "trick": I sit down and write a letter or email to someone (a friend, a client, a colleague) that explains in plain language what I know and believe about the subject. That helps me find the plain truth rather than working to get it right or "academic" or whatever.

Try telling your idea to someone else who has no knowledge of the subject but is an intelligent, good listener. Have him or her take notes on the main points heard. Then go over the notes. If he or she misunderstood, you haven't been clear. Go back and clarify the misunderstood points. You could also find a friend who, like me, has an outline-oriented mind and can listen to you and recite back a coherent outline of your idea and work.

Here is a seven-step outlining method I have taught many people. They have found it helpful. I wish I had learned this method when I started out. I think it would have been much easier to outline some of my books.

1. Make sure you focus your topic before you write.
2. Write down 15 words or concepts related to that topic.
3. Cull the words down to the best or most interesting 12 or so to make 12 chapter topics.
4. Beneath each chapter topic write out another 15 words or phrases.
5. Cut out the boring or repetitive words or phrases.
6. Turn the topics into questions, usually starting with the words: who, what, when, why, or how. (Insight: The human mind is predisposed to answer questions, so use the natural tendency that is already there.)
7. Do the same for subtopics: Find about 15 interesting words or phrases and turn them into questions and then write from the questions.

Some people use a mind map, a more visual way of outlining, in which they can put words or phrases in boxes or "clouds" that have connections with each other. There are books about how to create mind maps, and there is now some free or inexpensive software to draw your mind maps. If you are not such a linear thinker or do better when visualizing structures, this might be the best route for you to create your book outline.

This talk of outlining leads to my suggestion for structuring your nonfiction book. This works best for prescriptive nonfiction, self-help, or how-to books.

Suggested Structure of a Nonfiction Book

1. The introduction should have an origin story that conveys the passion of the writer and why the world needs this book.
2. Chapter 1 should have a clear statement of the problem and the promise of the book.
3. Chapter 2 should have an overview of the program/prescription that you are offering to deliver on the promise of the book.
4. The next chapters should be further explications of the program. If you have an acronym or a number of steps, these next chapters should each be about one of the steps or one of the letters in your acronym.
5. There might be some chapters on special applications of the program (with special populations or in special circumstances).
6. The final chapter should offer a summary of where you have been (problem, promise, and program) with something extra, such as a slightly different twist or suggestions for what to do next.

PLANNING YOUR WRITING TIME AND SCHEDULE

We have discussed this in detail in the chapter on getting your book written, but to put it in the context of this chapter, plan ahead for the best time in your schedule (as far in advance as you'd like) to write and finish your book.

PLANNING ON GETTING A LITERARY AGENT

If you are going for a big publisher that produces books for the general public, remember that you will almost certainly need an agent. Even if you have some connection to an editor at one of these publishing houses, he or she will want you to have an agent most of the time.

Compile a list of agents to contact. Look through your library or bookstore for similar books to yours. Check the acknowledgments sections to see if the authors thank their agents.

Look those agents up on the Internet or use the latest edition of Jeff Herman's book (*The Guide to Publishers, Editors, and Literary Agents*). Ask friends and colleagues if they know of anyone in the publishing world who might be willing to give you the name of an agent or one they know or who might help you make a connection with one.

Make a schedule of when you will send out queries and follow up if you haven't heard back. Start contacting the agents on your wish list, making dated notes on your actions and the responses. Go down the list until you get a nibble or a bite. Follow up right away to any response with an email or a letter.

Be persistent but not obnoxious. Be professional. Be courteous. Don't take rejections personally.

Here is a sample query letter you could adapt to contact an agent for representation.

Date
Dear Agent's name:

I am seeking literary representation for my book project, called [fill in the title and subtitle of your book—do not mention more than one book in your query letter].

The book is [fill in your high-concept and unique slant here, mentioning the genre, for example, mystery, self-help, motivational, how-to, prescriptive nonfiction. Also add a brief platform statement. Also add any supporting statistics that show the size and interest of the potential book buying audience in this kind of book].

I have contacted you since you represented [provide a book title that the agent represented and you admired or thought was well done if this is applicable; this shows that you have done your homework and are not just contacting a generic agent—if not, leave out this whole sentence], *a book I admire and thought was in the same ballpark as mine. If this idea and my query interest you, let me know and I can send along a proposal and some sample writing. If not, thank you for the time you spent considering it. I imagine you are very busy and appreciate the consideration. If I haven't heard from you in a few weeks, I will write again just to make sure my material arrived. If I still don't hear back from you, I will assume it is not a good fit. No need to return my materials—that would just add to your busy schedule.*

Sincerely,

PLANNING TO CONTACT A PUBLISHER OR EDITOR DIRECTLY

If you are going for a smaller or professional press, you won't need an agent and can query the publisher or an editor at the publishing house directly.

Get a list of publishers or editors whom you will contact. Look through your library or bookstore for similar books to yours and notice who publishes them.

Look that publisher up on the web or use Jeff Herman's book. Or ask friends and colleagues if they know of anyone in the publishing world who might be right for you to contact.

Make a schedule of when you will send out queries and follow up if you haven't heard back. Start contacting editors on your wish list, making dated notes on your actions and the responses. Go down the list until you get a nibble or a bite. Follow up right away to any response with an email or a letter.

Be persistent but not obnoxious. Be professional. Be courteous. Don't take rejections personally.

I send my query letters by email or by overnight package (I find it gets more attention). That's your call. Remember that your letter should have no typos and should be printed on nice paper. Do not handwrite any addresses on the envelope.

PLANNING ON SELF-PUBLISHING

Self-publishing is where planning is really necessary, because you are essentially becoming the "general contractor" for your book, much like you would be if you took on the task of building or remodeling a house.

In both cases, you wouldn't do all the tasks yourself, because no one can be a jack of all trades, but you would hire, outsource, and coordinate the efforts of many subcontractors to get the job done.

There are cover artists, editors, designers, marketing experts, and so forth with whom you need to work directly, whether you self-publish digitally or in print.

Here are some steps for self-publishing to help in your planning:

1. Decide which service you will use to get your book published (the top choices as I write are Smashwords. com, BookBaby.com, Apple's iBooks, Kindle Desktop Publishing for e-books; Lulu or CreateSpace for print books). Each service will have "specifications" that you will need to know and follow to get your book published. It's best to investigate and follow these from the start to avoid problems down the road.
2. If editing and design help are not included in the service you choose, investigate who offers those services by using the Internet and self-publishing handbooks. I use elance.com, fiverr.com, and other outsourcing or work-for-hire services to get most self-publishing tasks done for a reasonable fee. Finding these folks and managing them is quite a task in itself, which is why the one-stop options some of the publishing services offer save

time and avoid some of the risk that comes with using unknown freelancers. The web and people who have already explored these services are your best friends in this part of the task. If this is your first time, get an all-in-one service or find a coach/mentor or read a book to keep you from going astray.

3. Plan your marketing campaign early on, long before the writing of the book is completed. This is why I recommended in an earlier chapter that even self-published authors create a proposal. That proposal contains your marketing plan, which you draw upon to ensure that your book gets noticed and found by readers when it is released.

PLANNING YOUR BOOK SELLING, PUBLICATION, AND PROMOTION TASKS AND TIMELINES

Get one of those big wall calendars and schedule in the times you plan to send out your query letters (if you are seeking a publisher or an agent), that you plan to finish your proposal, that you plan to write the book, that you plan to get an editor to edit the book, that you are going to find a designer for the cover and the inside of the book (if you are self-publishing), and when you will have the final manuscript done.

If you are self-publishing or e-self-publishing, there are additional tasks, such as finding the right publishing service or packager, uploading, proofing, and getting final printed copies.

Then, whether you are self-publishing or using a traditional publisher, you need to plan out your book promotion tasks and timelines. Of course, you should in some ways always be working on your book promotion in that you should be expanding your platform, but there are usually more specific activities related to the book release.

One of the most effective things to do is to make a "launch" out of your book. Notice what Apple does to create buzz and eager anticipation for its upcoming products. The company doesn't just send out a press release; instead, the launch is a real event. You can do something similar for your book launch.

Below, I have given you a plan for a successful book launch. This strategy has been used by many authors and it works relatively well to fantastically. Check it out and put it in your calendar. If you need someone to help you implement the technical aspects of this strategy, get a techie friend or family member or hire someone on elance.com or some other outsourcing help site.

Book Launch Promotion Strategy

Recently some enterprising authors have used a book launch strategy that helps propel them to the top of Amazon.com's best-seller list or at least gives them some good momentum for early sales. I have done the following for some of my books and have compiled this guide if you would like to try it.

PLAN THE PROMOTION

1. Get the cover image of the book as a jpeg.
2. Write a compelling description of the book and what benefits the readers will get from reading it.
3. Get a firm publication date from the publisher or printer and plan your launch as close to that date as possible.
4. Contact potential partners who can provide valuable bonuses in exchange for free publicity and also have email lists to which they can announce the launch (and free stuff for their email subscribers); explain the benefits: good publicity for them; a new market of people they wouldn't have reached; the opportunity to offer those people further free stuff for signing up for that person's email list; valuable free stuff in addition to your book for their subscribers or email recipients; the

opportunity to use their own Amazon.com Associates link to earn a little on each book purchase if they want (otherwise provide them with your link if they don't have an account). Ask those partners if they have any other people with lists and bonuses they might suggest.

5. Create an opt-in page for people who are interested in your book topic or niche area so that you have a good list of people to send the book launch information to; offer a free valuable gift for them (usually a free report) in exchange for their joining your list and giving you permission to email them; make sure they confirm their interest; do not spam people or assume they want your emails—this is illegal these days and could get you into trouble.

6. Get a separate and dedicated domain name for the launch site, preferably with the title of the book as the domain name (e.g., www.BecomingaPublishedTherapist. com), but if that one is already taken, use some variation on the book title such as www.BecomingaPublishedTher-apistbook.com or www.PublishedTherapist.com. You might also consider misspellings of the book's title (e.g., www.PubishedTherapist.com), purchase relevant sites, and then point those to the correct launch page.

7. Set up an Amazon.com Associates account to be able to get a referral fee (attach your link to the image of the book cover and the Order Now buttons you will put on your launch site). You could earn a little more than your royalties for each book with this strategy.

8. Create a website or blog at that domain as the main launch page with an image of the book, the description of the book and its benefits for readers and the bonus descriptions and offer. Put the book cover, your promo-tional copy, your bonus offerings with descriptions and images for each, and the "call to action" (what people who want to get the book and the bonuses should do) on that site/blog.

9. Prepare emails and banners for your partners and make a time schedule to send them emails and receive their materials for the launch. You will almost certainly have to remind some of them many times to get their stuff. Get firm commitments as to dates and actions promised.

THE STRUCTURE OF THE PROMOTION

1. You are going to offer anyone who buys the book on Amazon.com (or BN.com or the Apple iBookstore) and forwards you a copy of his or her receipt the opportunity to receive bonus content for no charge immediately (make this a digital publication).
2. Don't have too much bonus material; make sure content is relevant and valuable to the target audience for your book; make sure the combined value of the bonuses is worth more than the book purchase price—this makes buying the book a no-brainer, essentially free.
3. The offer should be for a specific day or limited time period (say, a week) to give the book momentum and buzz; you may even reach the top 100 list on Amazon.com, which leads the company to promote your book (make sure you take a screenshot of the page if you find that happens and use it in your future promotions and add it to the launch page).

LAUNCH THE PROMOTION

1. Write all your partners each day for a week before the launch, reminding them of the launch date, verifying their agreement to send out their emails in a timely manner, and re-sending them all the promotional materials; remind them of the benefits they will get from doing the mailing and participating in the promotion.
2. Have someone who hasn't been involved try out the whole process to make sure it works.

3. Send out your email to your list; send more content out as the momentum builds and announce any successes or moving emails you get; keep your partners updated as well (e.g., that 100 people have downloaded your free bonus material and been exposed to your work).

Planning your Media Publicity

I got on *Oprah* due to some effort from my publisher and due to a fluke. After I was on, I wanted to get back on, but by then, the producer I had worked with had moved on and I didn't have an inside contact any longer. I bought a book by the publicist Susan Harrow about getting on *Oprah* and, while I didn't succeed at getting that to happen again, I did learn something valuable from the book.

She suggested that instead of thinking about how the show could help you, you think about how you could help the show. You could design a whole *Oprah* episode with several experts on your topic area. Lay out the whole show segment by segment, modeling on how Oprah usually does her show.

This was such an obvious point, but it came as a revelation to me. People approach me all the time for favors and my attention, as I have become a bit well known and successful. I can only imagine how it is for the folks at *Oprah* or other media outlets.

If someone approached me and offered me a way to help them by helping me, I would be much more open to their approach. Remember the section about getting blurbs from well-known people? The key to success is to think of the individual you are approaching, how busy and inundated he or she is, and how you can make the process easy. I applied this lesson to good effect when I did other media that were easier to get on than *Oprah*.

When I set out to publicize my book *Thriving Through Crisis*, I prepared a sheet of questions and answers, with likely timings for the answers, that I could send ahead to radio interviewers. They really appreciated it and I got to have questions for which I had already prepared good answers to boot.

Here is the sheet I sent, emailed, or faxed ahead.

Possible radio interview questions for Bill O'Hanlon, for his book "Thriving Through Crisis":

Teaser: After the break, we'll be talking to author and therapist Bill O'Hanlon, whose new book, *Thriving Through Crisis: Turn Tragedy and Trauma Into Growth and Change*, promises to show us how to turn post-traumatic stress into post-traumatic success.

Intro: We're here with Bill O'Hanlon, the author of 24 books, who has been a therapist for 30 years and has been a guest on *Oprah* and other national television shows and whose newest book is *Thriving Through Crisis*.

Question 1: Bill, there's been more and more talk and more books telling us about post-traumatic stress. Yet your new book tells us that trauma doesn't have to lead to permanent scarring or post-traumatic stress. Why not?

Answer: Takes approximately 1 and 1/2 minutes.

[Bill explains the difference between crises and traumas that lead to growth and those that lead to making our lives worse and continued suffering. We have a choice about how we handle overwhelming crises and traumas.]

Question 2: So what are the things people can do to turn a tragedy into a growth experience?

Answer: Takes approximately 3 1/2 minutes.

[Bill gives listeners three things that make the difference between shrinking or withdrawing from life after a trauma and the alternative of positive growth and change. Connection: Do you make better and different connections with yourself and others in the wake of a trauma or not? Quick story about Ric, who thought he had a perfect life, which then came crashing down. He used the crisis to find out who he was and changed the direction of his life.

Compassion: Does the crisis lead you to develop compassion for yourself or others or do you become bitter and cynical? Rudy Giuliani, widely seen as a get-tough, uncompassionate mayor in NYC, was widely admired for his compassionate response to victims of 9/11 and their families. He attributed his ability to be compassionate to his recently having had prostate cancer.

Contribution: Does the crisis lead you to withdraw from the world or to reach out and help others? Candy Lightener started MADD after her daughter was killed by a serial drunk driver.]

Question 3: You say in your book that there are five strategies that people seem to use to turn a tragedy into positive growth. What are those?

Answer: Takes approximately 2 1/2 minutes.

[Bill gives these five principles:

1. When you discover you're riding a dead horse, dismount
2. Don't just do something, stand there
3. Listen deeply to your heart and soul
4. Reading, writing, rituals
5. Change your life and keep the change.]

Question 4: You say that writing can be helpful for people in crisis. Tell us more about that.

Answer: Takes approximately 2 minutes.

[Bill tells of research that shows that people who write for as little as 15 minutes a day for as few as 3–5 days have improved health and lives following their crises. Bill gives quick guidelines for how to make this writing the most effective.]

Question 5: How do we help others who are going through crises?

Answer: Takes 2 minutes.

[Bill gives these four simple ideas:

1) Have patience—the crisis typically won't last forever.
2) Listen deeply and don't provide answers or solutions too quickly—Let them have their crisis; just be there for them with compassion and understanding if you can.
3) Notice what works and what doesn't with them.
4) Don't let them do their crisis all over you—the Lesson of the Brick Wall.]

Question 6: Wow! How do you write 24 books?

Answer: Takes 2 seconds.

[Bill says, "Stop me before I write again!"]

Note: Feel free to improvise and tease. Bill has done many interviews and is happy to roll with the punches. He's lively, has a good sense of humor, and can give as good as he gets when the interviewer jokes or teases. Bill can also expand on or shorten his response to any of these questions as time permits.

Bill's essential phone numbers:

Home office: 505.XXX.XXXX

Cellphone: 505.XXX.XXX

Website: www.thrivingthroughcrisis.com or www.billohanlon.com

Planning a Blog Book Tour

Most authors don't have much money for hiring publicists, so a simple but effective method for publicizing your book is a blog book tour.

A blog is essentially an online column focused on some topic. There are many bloggers out there these days. And if they write regularly, like columnists do, they have to come up with content on a regular basis. This can be challenging. So most bloggers would welcome it if you approached them and offered to write a "guest blog entry" or undergo an interview with them on the topic of your book if it is relevant to their target audience.

You need to do some research. Do online searches for your topic and put in the word "blog" with the search. For example, if I were searching for bloggers for the topic of this book, I would put in "writing help blog," "writing coaching blog," "psychotherapy blog," or "psychotherapist blog." Experiment with various combinations of terms until you have come up with a list of about 20 bloggers who show up in the first 10 or 15 results on different search engines.

CHAPTER 7

The 10 Ps to Getting Your Book Written and Published

WE HAVE COVERED A LOT OF MATERIAL, so I wanted to give you this summary. It will take us back through the material in the book in a slightly different way and can help you organize your thoughts about writing your book and getting it published. I call this summary "the 10 Ps to getting your book written and published."

1. **Passion.** Where's your juice? What energizes you? What are you passionate about? What do you care about enough to sustain you through the process of writing and publishing and promoting a book? What pisses you off that you want to change or correct in the world or tell people about? What are you absolutely terrified about people reading that you would write if you told the truth?

2. **Problem.** What problem does your book address? Is this a problem people will really be motivated enough to buy a book about?

3. **Promise.** What promise does your book make about offering a solution or relief from the problem you are

addressing? What benefit are you offering readers? After they read your book, what will they know or be able to do that they couldn't before reading your book?

4. **Population.** Who, specifically, would potentially (and realistically) buy your book? It's really not everyone in the world, so think more narrowly. This will help focus the book and its tone, as well as later marketing. It will also help you sell the book to an agent or a publisher. If you have statistics (such as there were 6 million books about getting published sold in the United States last year alone and books about publishing typically stay in print for 9 years), use them to bolster your case for the existence, size, and motivation of your audience.

5. **Prescription/Program.** What do you have to offer that is a unique solution or way to solve the problem and deliver the promise? This is usually given in steps, strategies, methods, or stages and sometimes with a time element. The 10-step model to losing 10 pounds? A better marriage in 21 days? The 5 ways to predict premaritally the likelihood of your getting a divorce? The FIRM method of resolving impotence? These could be themes as well. This 10 P model I am offering here is an example of a program or prescription.

6. **Platform.** Collect physical evidence of anything you have accomplished related to your specific topic or field or in general in your field and/or the accumulated evidence of your experience and ability to write books and sell them. This could include endorsements from well-known people.

7. **Position.** Your book idea and/or approach must be unique. It must fill a niche in the market no one else has found. You have to find a particular and compelling slant or angle on the subject, show that there is a population that is not being served by the existing books out there, and that potential readers will be motivated to buy the book. You might mention a tie-in with a news event or

trend. You might have a different program or prescription from all the other books on the subject. In any case, you must stand out from the crowd.

8. **Proposal.** The proposal is your sales tool and calling card for your book. It is like a brochure for a workshop. It should clearly and compellingly tell people who read it what your book is about and why they should read it or buy it or represent you. It has a rationale and summary of the book and it describes who you are and what the potential market for the book might be.

9. **Polish.** The only way to write is to write. The rest is all talk and stories. It doesn't have to be good, or perfect, but get it down on paper. Fix it later, but get it written. Notice what you do instead of writing and stop doing that. Write instead. *Writing begets more writing*, says the writer Dennis Palumbo. Most good writing is rewriting and editing. Discover your best method of revising. Have friends read it. Read it out loud. Rewrite after you finish every page. Don't rewrite until you've finished the whole thing. Wait 4 months until you forget what you've written and then read it with fresh eyes if you can for editing.

10. **Plan.** Make a writing plan, a get-an-agent plan, a revision/editing plan, a marketing and platform-building plan, a self-publishing or getting-a-publisher plan and any other plans you need to take you from where you are through publication and getting the word out about your book once it's published.

And now for your bonus **11th P: Persistence.** I was clueless when I started my journey in publishing land, but I had one thing going for me in addition to my passion. I was persistent. I wish I had had a book like this to help guide me along the way. Instead I stumbled along, working out the way as I went, visiting some dead ends and blind alleys. But eventually I got there. I got my first book published. And then some more. If

I, not a natural writer, a bit flakey, a professional-level procrastinator, and so on, can get a book written and published, I am convinced that almost anyone can. But you need to persist. Winston Churchill once exhorted the British people to "never, ever, give up." I give you the same exhortation. If you have a dream of writing and publishing a book, then follow the guidelines in this book, be willing to be edited and make adjustments as you go, and you will get there if you persist.

And another thing, before I let you go (you're going to go write, right?). Remember that the publishing industry and book readers need you. The publishing industry needs to constantly put out new books in order to make a profit and attract readers. They need new authors, new topics, and fresh slants on old topics. Readers are always looking for something to solve their problems, help them realize their dreams, pass the time, or entertain them.

Why shouldn't your book be among the next ones that get released into the world? No reason I can think of. Tell them all about it.

Ten Pieces of Advice From a Nonfiction Editor

I am Bill O'Hanlon's editor at Norton Professional Books, and here I offer a professional book editor's perspective for psychotherapists, detailing common mistakes and how to avoid them as well as advice for increasing one's likelihood of success in querying publishers. — Deborah Malmud

1. Please don't contact us by telephone. It's almost impossible to get our attention with a verbal description of a project—we need to know how you write. Also, few people like to be interrupted at work by someone whom they don't know. Calling us can get things off to a bad start. Don't risk it.

2. Instead . . . request (via email or a letter) our book proposal guidelines and then follow them to the letter. Don't skip over something that is requested and assume we just won't care. And don't decide to modify the guidelines to suit what you've got. For example, if the guidelines request a sample chapter, don't send us anything but a sample chapter. A blog post or article is not a suitable substitute.

3. Remember that editors specialize in what they acquire and publish. Don't send us something that is outside of our area of interest hoping that it will catch our eye. Doing so is a waste of everyone's time.

4. Your book proposal should not say that there is "no competition" for the book you are writing. This doesn't make us think your book is unique; it makes us think there is no market for it.

5. Your book proposal should not say that the readership is "everyone." No book has a readership of "everyone." Show us you understand who your potential readers are by clearly specifying who they are.

6. Think carefully before writing to us and saying that "so-and-so suggested I contact you." If "so-and- so" is an author of ours whose book is not doing well, or brings up a negative feeling, invoking his or her name might not be helpful.

7. Don't send a cover letter saying that another editor suggested you contact us. This indicates that the other editor already rejected your project and that we weren't the first publisher you contacted.

8. Don't resubmit something that we rejected a while ago hoping that (a) we've forgotten we rejected it or (b) the outcome will be different this time. Instead, spend the energy getting the book published elsewhere (or self-publishing) and then send an entirely new proposal if you want to contact us again.

9. Do write a short cover letter. It should explain what the book is about (one sentence) and who it is written for (one sentence), and state something very short (and hopefully impressive) about you. Long, involved cover letters about you and why you decided to write the book tend not to sit well with editors. The bulk of what you send should be the book proposal and writing sample.

10. If we reject your manuscript, assume we have done so because we don't think we are the right people for it—don't assume this means you will never get it published. Instead, move on and send the proposal to someone else. Whatever you do, don't lose confidence in your own work!

Deborah Malmud is a vice president at W. W. Norton & Company, Inc., and editorial director of Norton Professional Books.

Resources for Writers

Books

Herman, Jeff. (2011). *Jeff Herman's Guide to Book Publishers, Editors, and Literary Agents 2012.* Naperville, IL: Sourcebooks.

Herman, Jeff, and Deborah M. Adams. (2001). *Write the perfect book proposal: 10 that sold and why.* New York, NY: John Wiley and Sons.

Lamott, Anne. *Bird by Bird.* (1995). New York, NY: Anchor.

Zinsser, William. *On Writing Well.* New York, NY: Harper, 1998.

Websites

- Website for this book:
  www.BecomingaPublishedTherapist.com

- Google Keyword Research Tool:
  https://adwords.google.com/o/KeywordTool

- Sites for help with technical matters:
  www.elance.com
  www.fiverr.com

- Self-publishing sites:
  Kindle Desktop Publishing (https://kdp.amazon.com/)
  Book Baby (www.bookbaby.com)
  Smashwords (www.smashwords.com)
  Lulu (Lulu.com)

Index